THE SACRED PAUSE

*REST, PRESENCE, AND RECLAIMING
SELF-WORTH
(PART 2 OF THE UNHELD SERIES)*

GERALD E. O.

Table of Contents

Table of Contents 2
A Note to the Reader 6
    Day 100: No More Rushing 12
    Day 102: 20
    I Am Allowed to Pause 20
    Day 105: Anchored in Now 32
    Day 106: Rest Is a Right 36
    Day 108: Guilt-Free Rest 45
    Day 109: Sacred Slowness 49
    Day 110: 53
    Recovery, Not Resentment 53
    Day 111: The Healing in Doing Nothing 57
    Day 112: Rest as Resistance 62
    Day 113: 66
    Worth Is Not Performance 66
    Day 115: 74
    I Am Not What I Produce 74
    Day 116: 78
    Healing the Inner Prover 78
    Day 119: Born Worthy 91
    Day 120: Bracing for What's Not Coming 95
    Day 121: Hyper-vigilance Isn't Peace 100
    Day 122 – Honoring the Body's Story 105
    Day 123 – Learning Safety From Within 110
    Day 126: Rewriting My Baseline 122
WEEK 19 – Breathing Room: Giving Yourself Permission to Just Be 126

Day 127: The Space between Doing 126
Day 130: Permission to Be Unproductive 141
Day 133: Peace Is a Muscle Too 154
WEEK 20: Rest as a Form of Resistance 158
Day 134 – The Lie of Constant Productivity 158
Day 137 – The Nervous System Doesn't Lie 171
Week 21: "The Quiet Work of Healing" 190
Day 141: Healing Without Headlines 190
Day 142: The Work Behind the Smile 194
Day 143: Invisible Milestones 198
Day 144: Breaking Generational Echoes 202
Day 145: Healing Without a Finish Line 206
Day 147: The Day Nothing Hurts 214
Week 22: "Rest Is Not Retreat" 218
Day 148: Rest Without Guilt 218
Day 149: The Pause That Saves 222
Day 150: 226
Sacred Laziness 226
Month 5 Reflection: Growth Checkpoint 230
Day 152: The Fear of Falling Behind 234
Day 153: The Body Remembers 238
Week 23: "Grounding Through Nature" 246
Day 155: Earth Beneath Me 246
Day 156: My Place in the Wild 250
Day 157: Sky Above, Peace Within 253
Day 158: The Healing Wind 257
Day 159: My Nervous System in Nature 261
Day 160: Fire and Softness 265
Day 161: A Quiet Place Within 269

Week 24: "Let That Sh*t Go: Perfectionism" 273
    Day 162: The Myth of Being Enough.................................273
    Day 163: Permission to Mess Up 277
    Day 164: The Weight of Control...281
    Day 165: Flaws Are Part of the Story................................285
    Day 166: The Productivity Trap 289
    Day 167: Good Enough Is Enough 293
    Day 168: I Am Already Becoming......................................297
Week 25: Reclaiming Emotional Intimacy...................................301
    Day 169: Seen, Not Just Strong..301
    Day 170: The Courage to Be Known 305
    Day 171: The Cost of Withholding.....................................309
    Day 172: Let Love In 313
    Day 173: Vulnerability Is Strength.....................................317
    Day 174: Intimacy Requires Integrity 321
    Day 175: Emotional Intimacy Begins With Me 325
Week 26: Unlearning The Hustle Trap..329
    Day 176: Remembering Brotherhood...............................329
    Day 177: Competitive by Default.......................................333
    Day 178: Where Did All the Friends Go? 337
    Day 179: Emotional Fluency Among Men 341
    Day 180: Reaching Out...345
    Day 181: Holding Space for Another Man 349
    Month 6 Reflection: Mid-Year Mirror 353
Week 27: Expressing Without Fixing..358
    Day 183: You Don't Have to Fix It 358
    Day 184: When We Minimize Our Pain 362
    Day 185: Let It Be Messy...366
    Day 187: Listening Without Solving...................................374
    Day 188: Vulnerability Isn't Weakness 378

Day 189: Unlearning the Fixer Role 382
WEEK 28: Masculinity Without Control 386
    DAY 190: Let Go of the Grip 386
    DAY 194: Holding Space for Discomfort 407
    DAY 196: Rewriting Masculine Power 416
    Day 197 – The Myth of Hardness 420
    Day 203 – Returning to Your Natural State 451
    DAY 204: Words That Built My Armor 456
    DAY 208: Silences That Hurt 476
    DAY 211: The Cost of Carrying Others 488
    Day 216: The Fear of Being Alone 510
    Day 218: The Mask I No Longer Need 518
    Day 220: The Power of Saying What I Mean 527
    Day 222: Being Seen Is Not Weakness 535
    Day 225: When We Stopped Hugging 547
    Day 226: Unspoken Grief 553
Day 228: Rewriting Masculine Bonds 562
Day 229: I Miss Him 567

A Note to the Reader

This is not your typical journal.

This isn't about "fixing" you, improving your productivity, or turning you into some hyper-masculine ideal. This is a journal for the man who has carried too much, said too little, and felt unseen in the process. It's for the man who performs strength so well, no one notices when he's breaking inside.

Maybe that man is you.

UNHELD is a safe place — not to be perfect, but to be *present*. It's here to remind you that you are allowed to feel, to unravel, to be unsure, to rest, to breathe. You are allowed to want softness. You are allowed to want more.

Each page of this journal was written with you in mind. Not the version of you that holds it together for everyone else
— but the one underneath. The one who aches for peace. The one who just wants to be heard.

You're not alone here. Welcome home to yourself.

Why This Journal Exists

For generations, men have been taught to hold it in.

We've inherited silences. We've worn masks so long they feel like skin. We've confused numbness for strength, isolation for pride, and exhaustion for worth. Somewhere along the way, we lost access to our full humanity — and with it, the tools to heal.
This journal was born from that ache.

UNHELD exists because men deserve a space to feel without judgment. To explore their minds and emotions without the burden of performance. To practice mindfulness in a way that is both powerful and practical. To unlearn, reframe, and reconnect.

It exists because silence is no longer sustainable — and your wholeness matters.

How to Use This Journal

You'll find **365 days** of intentional reflection — one for each day of your year. You can begin in January or July, on your birthday or after a breakdown. There's no wrong time to start showing up for yourself.

Each daily page includes:

A *Mindful Insight* to challenge, ground, or inspire you. A *Prompt* to guide your reflection.

A *Mindful Minute* to pause and breathe.

An *Unheld Moment* — a truth, observation, or tension you may relate to.

Space to *journal freely* — for your thoughts, emotions, questions, or prayers.

At the end of each month, you'll find a **Monthly Reflection Page** to track your emotional growth, celebrate the unseen, and center your next steps.

You'll also have special pages for:

Letters You Never Sent — things you've always wanted to say.

Your Emotional Toolbox — practical coping tools and grounding techniques.

Daily Mantras — powerful affirmations for presence, softness, and strength.

Dreams, Goals & Visions — a space to imagine with no deadlines.

Coloring & Release Pages — spaces for creative expression and emotional release.

Use this journal daily, weekly, or whenever you need it. Let it be what it needs to be — some days a mirror, some days a friend.

What It Means to Be "Unheld"

To be **unheld** is to be strong in public and shattered in private.
It's the feeling of being praised for resilience no one helped
you build.
It's knowing how to support others but not how to ask for
support.
It's being so used to surviving, you forget what living feels
like.

But this journal reclaims the word.

To be *unheld* here is not a flaw — it's a beginning. It's the quiet truth that healing is overdue.
It's a man deciding that numbness is not his legacy.

This is not the end of you holding it together.
It's the beginning of you holding *yourself* — with grace.

Daily Reflection Structure

Every daily page in this journal is intentionally structured to support mindful masculinity — a balance of awareness, softness, and strength. Here's what to expect each day:

- Mindful Insight
  A daily observation, principle, or invitation rooted in mindfulness and emotional awareness.
- Reflection Prompt
  A thought-provoking question or prompt that encourages you to go inward and speak your truth.
- Mindful Minute
  A quick grounding practice — breathwork, stillness, gratitude, or presence. One minute is enough.
- Unheld Moment
  A relatable tension, truth, or struggle men carry but rarely name. You're not alone in this.
- Daily Journaling Space
  Blank space to write. No rules. Use it to vent, affirm, question, dream, or simply *be*.
- Quarterly Progress Markers
  At every 3-month interval, you'll pause for a deeper reflection — to honor your journey so far, reset your focus, and track your emotional evolution.

Day 100: No More Rushing

I've spent years sprinting through life—
chasing approval, dodging pain, proving my worth.

But healing doesn't happen in a
hurry. Peace doesn't live in panic.
And becoming myself is not a race.

Today, I choose a different rhythm.
I slow down, breathe deeper, and move with intention. There is no prize for burning out.

No more rushing.
I deserve to arrive fully in my own life.

Morning Reflection:

The rush to be "better" often comes from the lie that I'm not already whole.

Prompt:

- **Where in my life am I rushing myself to heal, grow, or achieve?**

_____
_____
_____
_____
_____
_____
_____
_____

Mindful Minute:

Breathe in this phrase: "I am not behind." Let it settle into your nervous system.

Mantra:

"I don't need to race toward healing. I am arriving every day."

Evening Reflection:

- **What pressure did I release today — even momentarily?**

_____
_____
_____
_____
_____
_____
_____

Day 101: Busy Isn't Always Brave

Staying busy gave me cover —
from grief, from questions, from myself.

I mistook constant motion for
strength, as if exhaustion meant I
mattered more.

But bravery isn't in how much I juggle
— it's in the pause, the "no," the
boundary, the choice to rest before I
break.

Today, I honor the courage it takes
to be still when the world tells me to keep going.

Morning Reflection:

Sometimes I stay busy to avoid myself. Stillness doesn't scare me anymore.

Prompt:

- **What am I keeping myself "too busy" to feel or face?**

_____
_____
_____
_____
_____
_____
_____
_____

Mindful Minute:

Turn off all distractions. Sit with yourself in silence. Notice what arises.

Mantra:

"I am not afraid of my own company."

Evening Reflection:

- **Was there a moment today when I chose presence over distraction?**

_____
_____
_____
_____
_____
_____
_____

Day 102:
I Am Allowed to Pause

There is no medal for running on empty. No honor in ignoring the body's whispers until they become screams.

I was taught that rest must be earned — after the work is done, after everyone else is okay.

But I am learning that
pausing isn't laziness,
it's wisdom.

A moment of breath
can be the most revolutionary thing I do today.

Morning Reflection:

Rest isn't earned — it's needed. It's human. It's holy.

Prompt:

- **Where do I feel guilty for needing rest, space, or quiet?**

_____
_____
_____
_____
_____
_____
_____
_____
_____

Mindful Minute:

Repeat internally: "I give myself permission to pause." Inhale. Exhale.

Mantra:

"Rest is my right, not a reward."

Evening Reflection:

- Did I allow myself to pause today — mentally or emotionally?

_____
_____
_____
_____
_____
_____
_____
_____

Day 103: Peace Over Performance

For so long, I measured my
worth by how well I could
perform— how useful I was,
how impressive I seemed.

But all that striving left
me tired, hollow,
disconnected from
myself.

Now, I am choosing
peace. Not the applause.
Not the approval.
Just the quiet
knowing that I am
enough,
even when no one is watching.

Morning Reflection:

If I must perform to be loved, that love is not peace. I choose peace.

Prompt:

- **Where in my life do I perform instead of being real?**

_____
_____
_____
_____
_____
_____
_____
_____

Mindful Minute:

With each breath, let go of the need to prove anything.

Mantra:

"I choose peace over perfection."

Evening Reflection:

- **How did I let myself just *be* today?**

_____
_____
_____
_____
_____
_____
_____
_____

Day 104: Slow Is Sacred

In a world that worships speed,
slowing down can feel like
failure. But there is wisdom in
stillness,
a depth that rush can never touch.

Slowness invites
clarity. It welcomes
presence.
It asks you to notice —
how you feel, what you
need, who you're
becoming.

You are not behind.
You are not wasting time.
You are honoring the sacred rhythm of your own
becoming.

Slow is not
weak. Slow is
sacred.
Let it be enough.

Morning Reflection:

Slow doesn't mean lazy. It means deliberate. Gentle. Present.

Prompt:

- **What area of my life needs a gentler, slower approach?**

_____
_____
_____
_____
_____
_____
_____
_____

Mindful Minute:

Do one thing slowly today — drinking water, walking, brushing your teeth — with full presence.

Mantra:

"My pace is sacred."

Evening Reflection:

- **What felt different about moving more slowly today?**

Day 105: Anchored in Now

So much of your mind has lived in two
places: the weight of the past
and the fear of the future.

But the present — this very moment —
is the only place where healing can take root.

Here, your breath is steady.
Your body is safe.
Your worth is intact.

You don't have to solve
everything. You don't have to
outrun anything.

You just have to *be*
— anchored in now.

Morning Reflection:

The future can wait. Right now, this moment, is all I have
— and that's enough.

Prompt:

- **How often do I leave the present moment?**

_____
_____
_____
_____
_____
_____
_____
_____

Mindful Minute:

Bring attention to five things you can see, four you can touch, three you can hear, two you can smell, one you can taste.

Mantra:

"I am here. I am now. I am safe."

Evening Reflection:

- **When did I feel most anchored in the present today?**

_____
_____
_____
_____
_____
_____
_____

WEEK 16: Redefining Rest

Rest isn't a luxury — it's a radical return to self. This week, we challenge the conditioning that equates rest with laziness. We begin to see rest as a form of rebellion, recovery, and restoration.

Day 106: Rest Is a Right

Rest isn't a reward.
It's not a luxury or a weakness.

It's a right.
A rhythm your body remembers,
even when the world tells you to keep pushing.

You are allowed to
stop. To breathe.
To just *be*.

You don't need to prove you're tired
enough. You already deserve rest.

Morning Reflection:

I don't have to earn my rest through burnout. I deserve it now, just as I am.

Prompt:

- What have I believed about rest that no longer serves me?

_____
_____
_____
_____
_____
_____
_____
_____

Mindful Minute:

Inhale: "I am allowed to rest."

Exhale: "I release the guilt."

Mantra:

"Rest is not a pause in progress — it is part of it."

Evening Reflection:

- **How did I give myself permission to rest today?**

_____
_____
_____
_____
_____
_____
_____
_____
_____

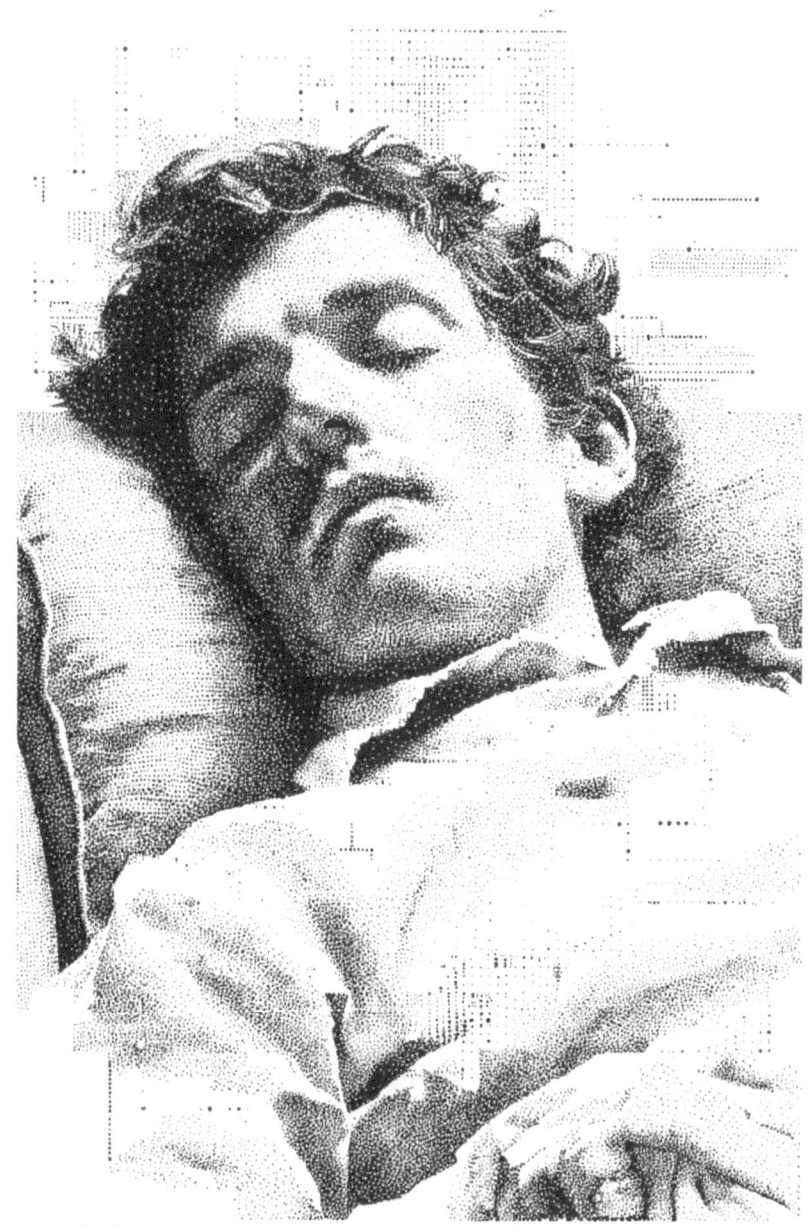

Day 107: The Rest That Actually Restores Me

Not all rest is
restorative. Scrolling
isn't stillness. Silence
isn't always peace.
Isolation isn't the same as solitude.

The rest that restores me…
is the kind that lets me exhale.
That loosens the grip of tension in my
jaw, softens the armor around my
chest,
and reminds my nervous system it is safe.

Rest isn't just about doing less —
it's about *being held more* deeply by what heals.

Today, I choose rest that actually reaches me.

Morning Reflection:

Not all rest is equal. Scrolling isn't soothing. What nourishes me at my core?

Prompt:

- **What kind of rest do I actually need today — physical, emotional, mental, or spiritual?**

_____
_____
_____
_____
_____
_____
_____
_____

Mindful Minute:

Close your eyes.

Ask your body: *What kind of rest do you need from me today?*

Mantra:

"Real rest is restoration — not distraction."

Evening Reflection:

- **Did I offer myself the kind of rest I truly needed today?**

_____
_____
_____
_____
_____
_____
_____
_____

Day 108: Guilt-Free Rest

I don't have to earn rest.
I don't need to prove exhaustion to deserve a break.

Rest is not
laziness. It is
reclamation.
A return to rhythm.
A reminder that I am not a machine.

The world may reward overwork,
but my body keeps score of what I ignore.

Today, I rest —
not out of permission from
others, but out of love for
myself.

Morning Reflection:

I don't have to apologize for needing space, sleep, or silence.

Prompt:

- **Where in my life do I feel I must "justify" taking breaks?**

_____
_____
_____
_____
_____
_____
_____
_____

Mindful Minute:

Visualize guilt leaving your body like smoke with each exhale.

Mantra:

"My rest is valid. My healing is sacred."

Evening Reflection:

- **What guilt did I release today, if only for a moment?**

_____
_____
_____
_____
_____
_____
_____

Day 109: Sacred Slowness

Everything doesn't have to happen fast to be meaningful. Slowness is not stagnation — it's depth.

In the quiet pace,
I hear myself more clearly.
I move with intention, not impulse.

I've spent years rushing to
arrive. Now, I want to dwell in
the journey.

Sacred slowness reminds
me: I'm not behind.
I'm becoming.

Morning Reflection:

Slowing down is not falling behind. It's remembering I am not a machine.

Prompt:

- **What does sacred slowness mean to me — and how can I honor it today?**

_____
_____
_____
_____
_____
_____
_____
_____

Mindful Minute:

Walk or breathe slowly today — intentionally. Feel your pace return to you.

Mantra:

"I am not behind. I am in rhythm with myself."

Evening Reflection:

What did I notice when I moved more slowly?

Day 110:
Recovery, Not Resentment

I used to push through pain,
then resent myself for
breaking.

But healing isn't weakness.
Recovery is not a setback — it's a sacred return.

Today, I choose to honor my
limits without shame.

To pause without
guilt. To recover, not
resent.

Because rest is not just restoration —
it's resistance to the cycles that once drained me.

Morning Reflection:

When I ignore my need to rest, I don't become stronger — I become bitter.

Prompt:

- **Have I been pushing myself past my capacity lately? What's the cost?**

_____
_____
_____
_____
_____
_____
_____
_____

Mindful Minute:

Place your hands over your heart. Say inwardly: "I see your effort. I grant you recovery."

Mantra:

"I choose recovery, not resentment."

Evening Reflection:

- **Did I offer my body or mind a moment of recovery today?**

_____
_____
_____
_____
_____
_____
_____
_____

Day 111: The Healing in Doing Nothing

I don't always need a
plan. Or a solution.
Or a way to optimize the moment.

Sometimes, doing nothing
is exactly what my body, my mind, and my soul
need.

Stillness is not
laziness. It's
listening.
It's letting the world soften around
me so I can soften within.

Today, I give myself that gift —
without explanation, without
guilt.

Morning Reflection:

Doing nothing is healing when it's intentional. I am allowed to be.

Prompt:

- **Why does "doing nothing" feel so hard sometimes?**

_____
_____
_____
_____
_____
_____
_____
_____

- **What am I afraid will surface?**

_____
_____
_____
_____
_____
_____
_____
_____

Mindful Minute:

Sit or lie down. Let your body sink into wherever you are.
Just *be*.

No fixing.

No

forcing.

Mantra:

"There is healing in the quiet."

Evening Reflection:

- Was I able to be still without self-judgment today?

_____
_____
_____
_____
_____
_____
_____

Day 112: Rest as Resistance

In a world that demands I always
produce, rest becomes more than
recovery —
it becomes rebellion.

Rest says:
I am more than my
output. My worth is not
in my work. My
existence is enough.

Choosing rest is how I reclaim myself
from the systems that said I had to earn love.
It's how I honor my body, my mind, and my
boundaries.

Today, I rest —
not because I'm weak,
but because I'm finally strong enough to say no.

Morning Reflection:

In a world that demands constant productivity, my rest is resistance. It's radical self-care.

Prompt:

- **How does rest help me reclaim my humanity?**

_____
_____
_____
_____
_____
_____
_____

Mindful Minute:

Repeat softly: "I am not a machine. I am not a product. I am a person."

Mantra:

"My rest resists what tries to erase me."

Evening Reflection:

- **What part of me felt reclaimed in rest today?**

_____
_____
_____
_____
_____
_____
_____

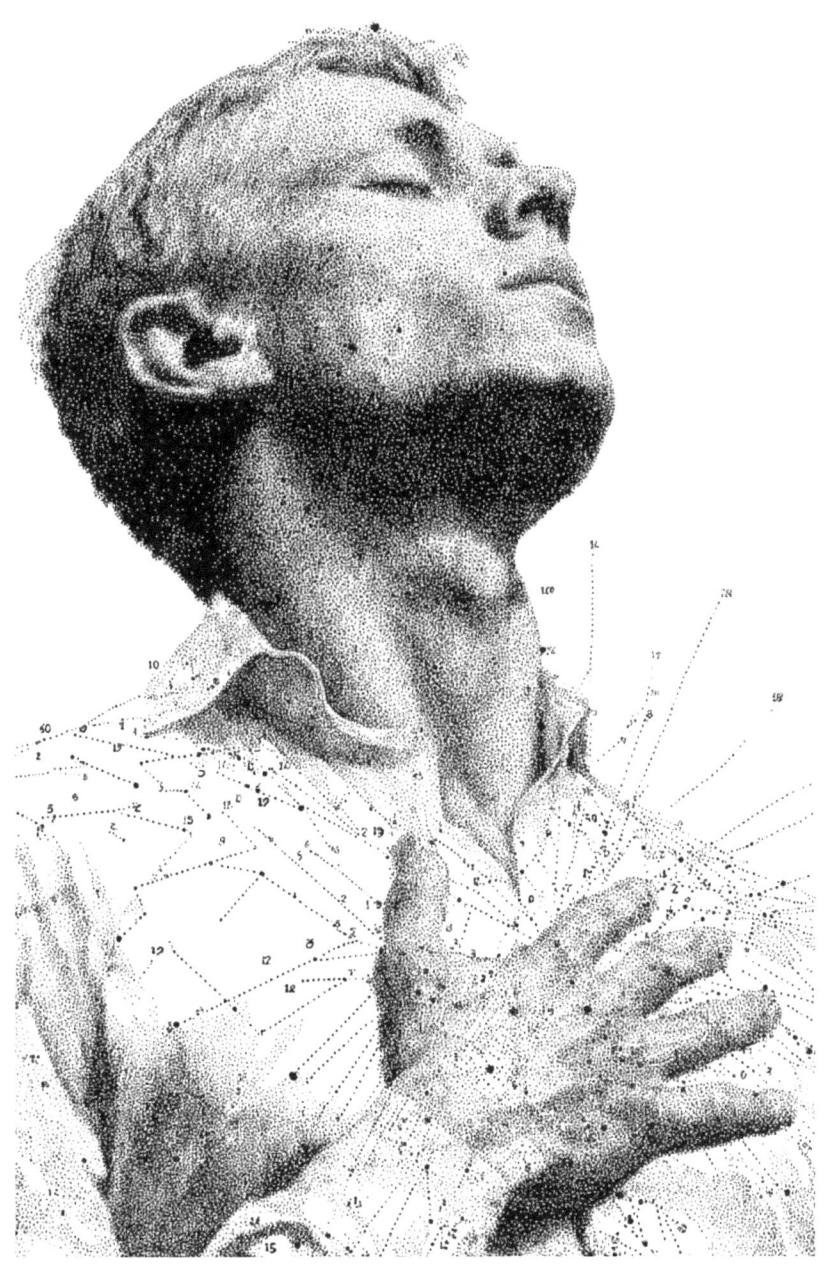

WEEK 17:
Stop Earning Your Worth

You were born worthy. Period. This week, we unhook from the lie that our value is something we must earn, prove, or beg for. It's already yours.

Day 113:
Worth Is Not Performance

I am not an actor on a
stage, measured by
applause, praised when I
please, dismissed when I
don't.

My worth is not in how well I
perform, how much I give,
or how little I need.

Even when I am quiet, unseen, or
still— I am worthy.

Even when I am tired, unsure, or
healing— I am enough.

Today, I remind myself:
I don't have to prove I
belong. I already do.

Morning Reflection:

My worth is not tied to how much I do or how well I do it. I am enough — even in stillness.

Prompt:

- **Where in my life have I confused achievement with worth?**

_____
_____
_____
_____
_____
_____
_____
_____

Mindful Minute:

Place your hand over your chest and say: "I am worthy because I exist."

Mantra:

"My worth is not up for debate."

Evening Reflection:

- **Did I notice myself trying to prove my worth today? How did I respond?**

Day 114: The Hustle Isn't Holy

They taught me that constant motion was
virtue— that exhaustion meant I was doing it
right,
that hustle was the sacred path to manhood.

But what if stillness is sacred
too? What if peace is just as
productive as pushing through
pain?

I am not a machine.
I am not defined by how much I can endure
before breaking.

The hustle may build
wealth, but it cannot build
wholeness.

Today, I choose sacred
slowness over performative
pressure.

Morning Reflection:

Burnout is not a badge of honor. Exhaustion is not
my destiny.

Prompt:

- **What do I fear would happen if I slowed down?**

_____
_____
_____
_____
_____
_____
_____
_____
_____

Mindful Minute:

Take three deep breaths. With each exhale, release one expectation placed on you.

Mantra:

"I don't need to break to be valued."

Evening Reflection:

- **Where did I challenge the hustle mindset today?**

_____
_____
_____
_____
_____
_____
_____
_____

Day 115: I Am Not What I Produce

Somewhere along the way,
my value got tangled up
in my output.

In achievements,
checklists, and how
useful I could be to
everyone but myself.

But I am not a
machine. I am not a
project.
I am not what I produce.

Even in stillness, I am worthy.
Even in rest, I belong.

Today, I remind myself:
being is enough.

Morning Reflection:

I am not a task list. I am not my paycheck. I am not the weight I carry.

Prompt:

- **What would be left of me if I stopped doing and simply *was*?**

_____
_____
_____
_____
_____
_____
_____
_____

Mindful Minute:

In stillness, repeat: "Who I am is enough." Let that truth settle into your bones.

Mantra:

"I am enough without performance."

Evening Reflection:

- Was I able to be present with myself today, without needing to earn it?

_____
_____
_____
_____
_____
_____
_____

Day 116:
Healing the Inner Prover

There's a voice inside me
that's always trying to
earn— love, approval,
belonging.

It whispers, *"Do more, be better, prove them wrong."*
It kept me alive once.
But now, it's keeping me tired.

Healing doesn't mean I no longer care.
It means I no longer need to prove
myself to feel like I matter.

Today, I thank that voice for its
service. And gently remind it:
I am already enough.

Morning Reflection:

The part of me that keeps trying to earn love is just trying to stay safe. I see him. I'll show him a better way.

Prompt:

- **What part of me still feels like it has to prove its worth?**

_____
_____
_____
_____
_____
_____
_____

- **Where did that come from?**

_____
_____
_____
_____
_____
_____

Mindful Minute:

Imagine that younger version of yourself — the one who tried so hard. Tell him: "You don't have to try anymore.
You're already enough."

Mantra:

"I don't need to prove. I just need to be."

Evening Reflection:

- **How did I offer grace to my inner prover today?**

_____
_____
_____
_____
_____
_____
_____
_____
_____

Day 117:
The Lie of "Not Enough"

Somewhere along the way,
I began to believe that who I am
is lacking—unfinished, unworthy,
incomplete. That to be loved, I had to
become someone else.

But "not enough" is a lie
passed down by wounded systems and
voices who didn't know better.

The truth is quieter but
deeper: I was always
worthy.
Even before I proved, performed, or
achieved. Even when I didn't believe it.

And today, I'm learning to believe it anyway.

Morning Reflection:

"Not enough" is a lie — and it's not mine to carry.

Prompt:

- **Who or what made me feel like I was never enough?**

_____
_____
_____
_____
_____
_____
_____
_____

- **How do I begin to unlearn that?**

_____
_____
_____
_____
_____
_____
_____
_____

Mindful Minute:

As you inhale, say: "I am enough."

As you exhale, say: "I release the lie."

Mantra:

"I release what was never mine to carry."

Evening Reflection:

- **What truth about myself did I reclaim today?**

_____
_____
_____
_____
_____
_____
_____
_____

Day 118 – Worthiness Without Witness

There are moments when no one sees your effort, no one applauds your healing, no one notices the quiet battles you've fought.

But worthiness was never meant to be proven under spotlights or in loud rooms.

It lives in the unseen spaces—
in how you keep showing up for yourself, in the gentleness you offer your own soul, even when no one is watching.

You are worthy,
not because the world says
so, but because you simply
are.

Morning Reflection:

Even if no one claps, I am still worthy. My value doesn't need validation.

Prompt:

- **How do I seek validation from others?**

  _____
  _____
  _____
  _____
  _____
  _____
  _____

- **What would it mean to validate myself instead?**

  _____
  _____
  _____
  _____
  _____
  _____
  _____
  _____

Mindful Minute:

Look into a mirror or close your eyes. Say: "You are enough, even when unseen."

Mantra:

"I don't need an audience to be valuable."

Evening Reflection:

- **Was I able to affirm myself from within today?**

_____
_____
_____
_____
_____
_____
_____
_____

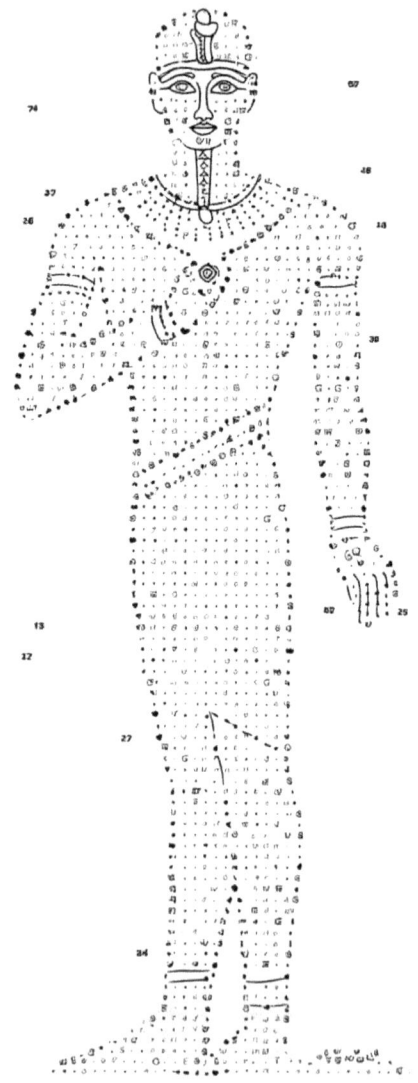

Day 119: Born Worthy

Before the striving,
before the
expectations,
before the world tried to reshape
you— you were already enough.

You didn't earn your worth.
You entered this world wrapped in it.

You were born worthy of
love, of safety, of softness,
of being held without having to perform.

And that truth has never
changed— only forgotten.

Today is a chance to remember.

Morning Reflection:

I arrived in this world already worthy. I don't need to hustle to return to that truth.

Prompt:

- What does it mean to believe I was born worthy?

_____
_____
_____
_____
_____
_____
_____

Mindful Minute:

Breathe deeply.

Let your breath anchor you in your worth. There's nothing to fix.

Mantra:

"I was born worthy. I will die worthy. I *am* worthy."

Evening Reflection:

- How did I show up today knowing I didn't have to earn anything?

_____
_____
_____
_____
_____
_____
_____

WEEK 18: My Nervous System Is Not a Warzone

This week is about learning to live in your body without constantly bracing for impact. You're not in danger anymore. It's time to come home to safety — within yourself.

Day 120: Bracing for What's Not Coming

Your shoulders
tighten. Your breath
shortens.
Your mind scans for
danger— even in moments
of peace.

Because for so long, calm was a
warning. Peace was a pause before the
storm.
Safety was unfamiliar, and therefore suspicious.

But maybe the threat isn't
here. Maybe it's just the
memory.
The body remembering what the mind has tried to
forget.

You don't have to brace
anymore. Not for pain that's
not coming.
Not for the worst that never arrives.

This moment is different.
Let yourself feel the difference.

Morning Reflection:

I've lived many days anticipating pain that never
arrived. I release the need to stay guarded.

Prompt:

- **Where in my body do I still hold tension from old battles?**

_____
_____
_____
_____
_____
_____
_____
_____
_____

Mindful Minute:

Place your hand on your heart. Whisper: "It's safe to exhale now."

Mantra:

"I am safe here. I don't need to brace anymore."

Evening Reflection:

- **What moment today reminded me I'm no longer in survival mode?**

_____
_____
_____
_____
_____
_____
_____

Month 4 Reflection: Looking Backward, Leaning Forward

- **Key Journal Excerpts or Memories That Stuck With Me**

    Skim through this month's entries.

    Highlight 1–2 passages, quotes, or

    insights.

Day 121: Hyper-vigilance Isn't Peace

Always scanning.
Always prepared.
Always a little tense — even in moments meant for joy.

You may have learned to stay alert because the world around you wasn't always safe.
Because someone had to be ready.
Because danger taught you to anticipate, to overthink, to carry it all.

But hyper-vigilance isn't
peace. It's survival stretched
too far.
It's your body doing its best to protect you — long
after the threat is gone.

Today, offer yourself another
way. A breath that doesn't
brace.
A pause that doesn't panic.
A reminder: You're allowed to feel safe now.

Morning Reflection:

Being alert 24/7 is not the same as being alive. I choose aliveness.

Prompt:

- **When did I first learn to constantly scan for danger?**

_____
_____
_____
_____
_____
_____
_____
_____

Mindful Minute:

Close your eyes and scan your body slowly.

Say: "You don't have to stay ready."

Mantra:

"I release the need to constantly prepare for pain."

Evening Reflection:

- **Was I able to soften my guard today — even just a little?**

_____
_____
_____
_____
_____
_____
_____
_____

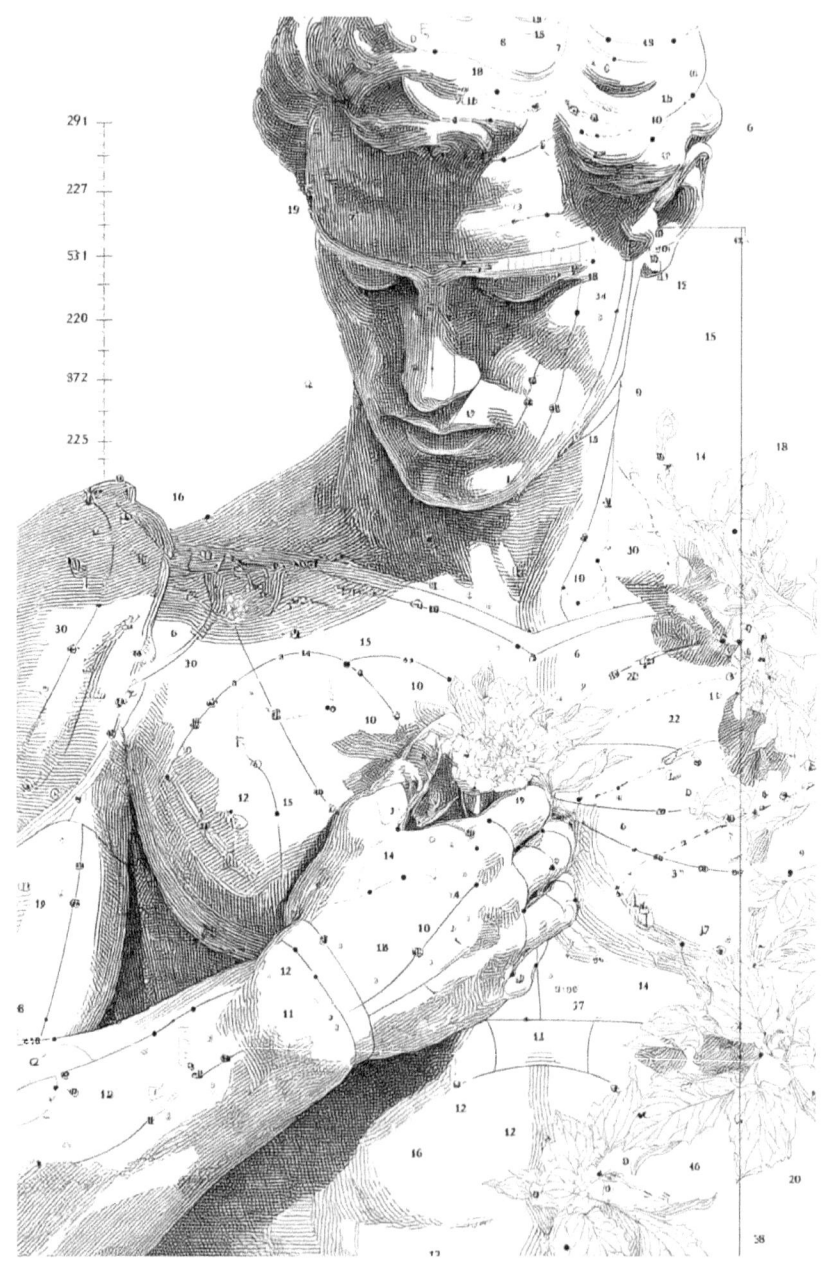

Day 122 – Honoring the Body's Story

Your body remembers.
Even the things your mind has tucked
away. It holds the tension of unshed
tears,
the fatigue of long-carried burdens,
the posture of always trying to be "enough."

But it also remembers laughter.
Softness.
Moments when you felt safe, whole, and seen.

This body — your body — has carried you through it
all. Instead of shame, offer it gratitude.
Instead of criticism, offer it compassion.

Honor the stretch marks, the scars, the
aches — not as flaws, but as records.
Proof that you have
survived. And that you're
still becoming.

Morning Reflection:

My body has witnessed every chapter of my life —
even the ones I've tried to skip. Today, I honor its
memory with care instead of shame.

Prompt:

- **If my body could write me a letter about what it's been through, what would it say?**

　_____
　_____
　_____
　_____
　_____
　_____
　_____
　_____

- **What would it ask for?**

　_____
　_____
　_____
　_____
　_____
　_____

Mindful Minute:

Place your hand on the part of your body that feels most tense. Whisper, "You've carried enough. I hear you."

Mantra:

"My body holds my story — not my punishment."

Evening Reflection:

- **Did I treat my body like a home or a battlefield today?**

_____
_____
_____
_____
_____
_____
_____
_____

Mantra:

"My body is not the enemy. It's my oldest ally."

Evening Reflection:

- **What did my body try to tell me today?**

_____
_____
_____
_____
_____
_____
_____
_____

Day 123 – Learning Safety From Within

Not all safety is external.
Sometimes, the walls you need
most are the ones built from trust
in yourself.

The world may not always feel safe
— but your breath can be a
sanctuary.
Your boundaries can be a
shield. Your truth can be a
compass.

You don't have to outsource security anymore.
You are learning to be a safe place for your own
heart. To soothe your fears,
to stay when it's hard,
to listen when pain speaks.

Safety, real safety, begins with you.

Morning Reflection:

Safety isn't always a location — it can be a sensation. I can build that inside myself.

Prompt:

- What practices help me feel safe inside my own skin?

_____
_____
_____
_____
_____
_____
_____
_____

Mindful Minute:

Place both hands on your stomach. Breathe deeply. Repeat: "I am grounded. I am safe. I am here."

Mantra:

"Safety begins with how I hold myself."

Evening Reflection:

- **How did I anchor myself in safety today?**

_____
_____
_____
_____
_____
_____
_____

Day 124: Calming the Alarm

Morning Reflection:

The world isn't always shouting. Sometimes it's me — my inner alarm. I can learn to turn the volume down.

Prompt:

- **What triggers still set off my inner alarm?**

_____
_____
_____
_____
_____
_____
_____
_____

- **Can I name them with compassion?**

_____
_____
_____
_____
_____
_____
_____

Mindful Minute:

Imagine a volume dial on your nervous system.
Lower it one notch with each breath.

Mantra:

"I am allowed to feel calm — without guilt."

Evening Reflection:

- **What brought my system peace today?**

_____
_____
_____
_____
_____
_____
_____
_____

Day 125: Gentle Is Powerful

Gentleness is not the absence of
strength — it's the presence of control,
awareness, and care.

It takes power to respond, not react.
To choose tenderness in a world that taught you
toughness. To hold space instead of holding back.

Gentle men aren't weak.
They are brave enough to lead with
heart. To speak with empathy.
To walk with intention.

You don't have to be harsh to be
heard. Gentle is still powerful.

Morning Reflection:

I grew up believing gentleness made me weak. But it's gentleness that's healing me.

Prompt:

- **What does being gentle with myself look like in daily life?**

_____
_____
_____
_____
_____
_____
_____
_____

Mindful Minute:

Stroke your own forearm gently for 30 seconds. Let your body register that soft is safe.

Mantra:

"Gentleness is not weakness — it's my return to wholeness."

Evening Reflection:

- **Did I practice gentleness today in how I moved, spoke, or thought?**

_____
_____
_____
_____
_____
_____
_____

Day 126: Rewriting My Baseline

What you called "normal" was often
survival. Bracing for conflict.
Anticipating disappointment.
Earning love through
performance.

But you don't have to live there

anymore. Safety doesn't need tension.
Love doesn't require proving.
Peace isn't earned — it's remembered.

You're allowed to rewrite your baseline
— from hypervigilance to calm,
from people-pleasing to
authenticity, from exhaustion to
ease.

What if your new normal was
gentler? More honest?
More you?

Morning Reflection:

My baseline doesn't have to be tension, reactivity, or numbness. I get to choose calm.

Prompt:

- **If peace were my default setting, how would I move through the world?**

_____
_____
_____
_____
_____
_____
_____

Mindful Minute:

Repeat: "My baseline is calm. I return to peace with every breath."

Mantra:

"Peace is my new normal."

Evening Reflection:

- **What's shifting in me as I make peace my home?**

_____
_____
_____
_____
_____
_____
_____

WEEK 19 – Breathing Room: Giving Yourself Permission to Just Be

There's a sacred kind of growth that happens when you're not striving, fixing, or performing — when you simply give yourself room to breathe. This week is about easing the grip, creating emotional space, and letting peace become your baseline, not a reward.

Day 127: The Space between Doing

In a world obsessed with
doing, being feels like
rebellion.
But between every
task, every goal,
every plan—
there is a sacred pause.

That space isn't empty.
It's where your breath
returns. Where clarity
visits.
Where your worth speaks,
without needing a
performance.

You are not just the things you
accomplish. You are the awareness that
holds them.

Let the space between
doing become a place of
becoming.

Morning Reflection:

Productivity is not proof of my worth. I am allowed to rest and still be enough.

Prompt:

- **What part of me panics when I slow down?**

_____
_____
_____
_____
_____
_____
_____

- **What story does it tell me?**

_____
_____
_____
_____
_____
_____
_____

Mindful Minute:

Close your eyes and take 5 slow breaths. With each exhale, say silently: "There is no emergency here."

Mantra:

"I am not what I produce. I am enough as I am."

Evening Reflection:

- Did I pause today without guilt?

_____
_____
_____
_____
_____
_____
_____

- What did that moment give me?

_____
_____
_____
_____
_____
_____
_____
_____

Day 128: Unlearning the Rush

You were taught to chase time—
to move fast, achieve faster, and always stay
ahead. But speed isn't always synonymous
with growth.
Sometimes, it's just a way to avoid stillness.

To unlearn the rush is to realize
that not everything meaningful can be
hurried. Healing takes time.
Becoming takes presence.

You don't have to live in a state of
urgency. You're not behind.
You're simply arriving—at your own pace.

Morning Reflection:

Rushing has become a reflex — not because
everything is urgent, but because urgency has become
a comfort zone.

Prompt:

- **Where in my life do I confuse speed with safety?**

_____
_____
_____
_____
_____
_____
_____
_____
_____

Mindful Minute:

Walk slowly around your space, paying attention to the sound of your feet. Let your body slow your mind.

Mantra:

"Slow is sacred. I trust the pace of peace."

Evening Reflection:

- **How did I invite slowness into at least one part of my day?**

_____
_____
_____
_____
_____
_____
_____

Day 129: Gentle is Not Weak

Gentleness has been
misunderstood— mistaken for
fragility, dismissed as soft. But
gentleness is a quiet strength,
a steady hand that doesn't need to grip tight to be
firm.

It takes courage to be calm in a world that
demands harshness.
It takes power to choose compassion over
control, to speak softly when anger rises.

Gentle doesn't mean
passive. It means rooted.
It means
sure. It
means safe.

Morning Reflection:

Gentleness is a radical act in a world that glorifies toughness. I am choosing inner softness over inner war.

Prompt:

- How was gentleness modeled (or not) in my upbringing?

_____
_____
_____
_____
_____
_____
_____
_____

- What did I learn about being "too soft"?

_____
_____
_____
_____
_____
_____

Mindful Minute:

Place a hand on your heart and breathe deeply. Say to yourself: "I'm safe to be gentle."

Mantra:

"My strength is not in the force I exert, but in the softness I allow."

Evening Reflection:

- **Did I show myself gentleness today?**

_____
_____
_____
_____
_____
_____
_____

- **How did it feel?**

_____
_____
_____
_____
_____
_____
_____

Day 130: Permission to Be Unproductive

You don't have to earn your rest.
You don't have to justify every quiet hour with future results.
You are not a machine —
you are a human being with needs beyond performance.

Some days, doing nothing is doing something. It's how you heal.
How you hear yourself again.
How you remember that your worth isn't tied to your output.

Today, give yourself permission to be unproductive — and still be enough.

Morning Reflection:

Rest is not a prize for hard work. It's a birthright.

Prompt:

- **What does "doing nothing" make me feel?**

_____
_____
_____
_____
_____
_____
_____
_____

- **What belief lies beneath that discomfort?**

_____
_____
_____
_____
_____
_____
_____
_____

Mindful Minute:

Set a timer for 60 seconds. Sit. Breathe. Do nothing but be.

Mantra:

"Doing nothing is still doing something for me."

Evening Reflection:

- **Where did I allow space for stillness — without justifying it?**

_____
_____
_____
_____
_____
_____
_____

Day 131: No One's Measuring

The timeline you're racing
against? The imaginary
scoreboard?
The invisible judge in your
head? They're not real.

There's no one keeping score of how fast you
heal, how much you achieve,
or how flawlessly you move through life.

Let that weight fall off your shoulders.
You're allowed to move at your own
pace. You're not behind —
you're on your way.

Morning Reflection:

I release the illusion that someone is always watching, grading, or keeping score.

Prompt:

- **Whose invisible expectations am I still trying to meet?**

_____
_____
_____
_____
_____
_____
_____
_____

Mindful Minute:

Imagine putting down a heavy backpack filled with other people's opinions. Feel how light you are.

Mantra:

"I live for truth, not for performance."

Evening Reflection:

- **When today did I show up for *me*, not for anyone else's approval?**

_____
_____
_____
_____
_____
_____
_____
_____

Day 132: I Don't Have to Earn My Breaths

You don't have to hustle for air.
You don't need to prove your right to rest.

Being alive is enough.
Worthy of love.
Worthy of peace.
Worthy of space.

Inhale
gently.
Exhale
shame.
You were never meant to earn what is already yours.

Morning Reflection:

I don't have to earn my existence. Breathing is proof that I belong here.

Prompt:

- **What would it look like to live as if I already deserve peace?**

_____
_____
_____
_____
_____
_____
_____
_____

Mindful Minute:

Breathe in slowly and say, "I deserve this." Breathe out slowly and say, "I am allowed to rest."

Mantra:

"My worth is not on trial. It never was."

Evening Reflection:

- Did I believe I deserved ease today?

_____
_____
_____
_____
_____
_____
_____

- **What did that change?**

  _____
  _____
  _____
  _____
  _____
  _____
  _____
  _____

Day 133: Peace Is a Muscle Too

Peace isn't always passive.
Sometimes it's the quiet
strength of choosing not to
react,
of softening in a world that demands hardness.

It takes practice —
to sit with
discomfort
without letting it define you.

Like a muscle, peace grows
each time you return to
yourself instead of the noise.

Morning Reflection:

Peace isn't something I stumble into — it's something I practice and strengthen.

Prompt:

- **What consistent habits could help make peace my default setting?**

_____
_____
_____
_____
_____
_____
_____
_____

Mindful Minute:

Stretch slowly for 1 minute. With each movement, repeat: "I choose peace."

Mantra:

"I am building a peaceful life, one breath at a time."

Evening Reflection:

- What helped me stay anchored in peace today — and when did I drift?

_____
_____
_____
_____
_____
_____
_____
_____

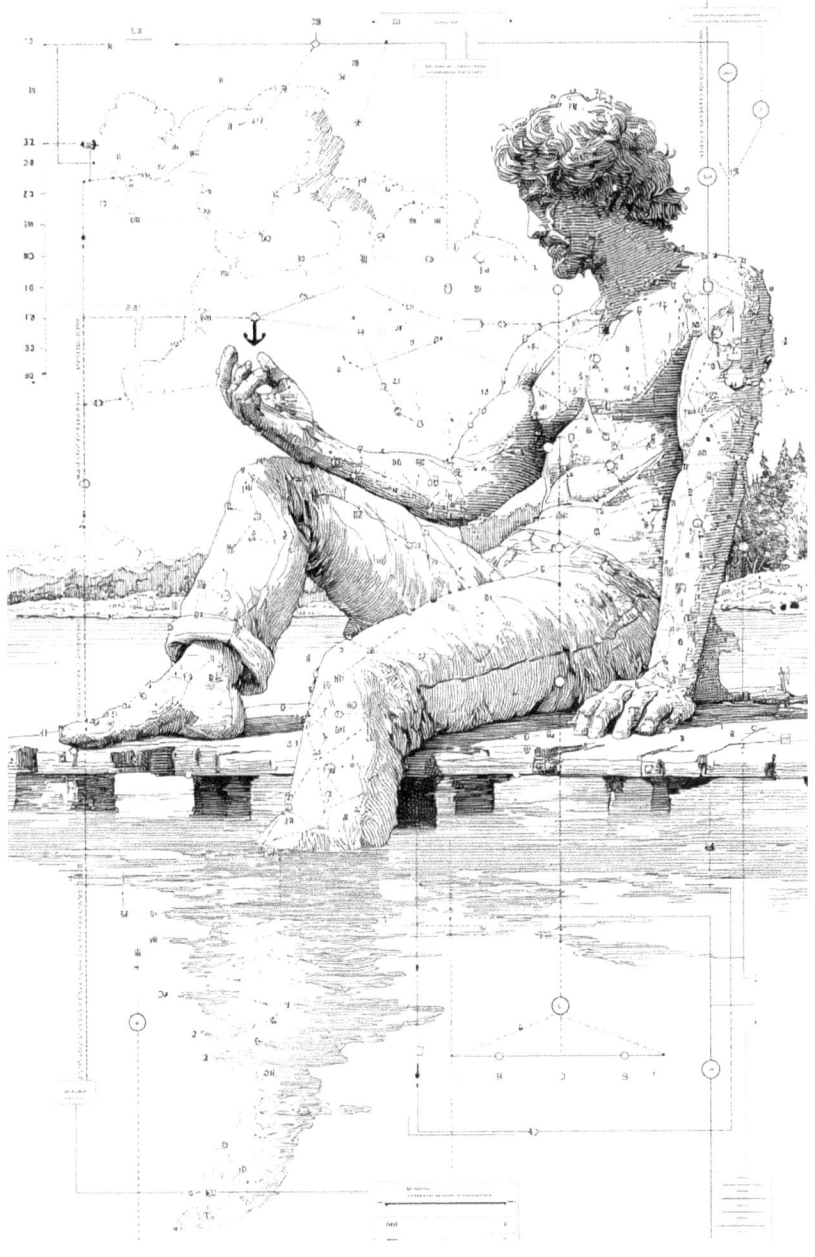

WEEK 20: Rest as a Form of Resistance

In a world that glorifies burnout and busyness, choosing rest can feel like rebellion. But rest isn't weakness — it's wisdom. This week is about redefining your relationship with rest. Not as something you earn, but as something you're inherently worthy of.

Day 134 – The Lie of Constant Productivity

You were taught to measure your
worth by how much you get done.
To believe that stillness is
laziness, and exhaustion is a
badge of honour.

But that's a lie.

You are not a machine.
Your value isn't tied to output.
Rest is not a reward — it's a rhythm.

Let yourself be
human. Let yourself
just be.

Morning Reflection

You are not a machine. You were never meant to be. What parts of you still tie your worth to how much you accomplish?

Prompt

- **What does productivity mean to you — and who defined it?**

_____
_____
_____
_____
_____
_____
_____
_____
_____

Mindful Minute

Sit in stillness and repeat: *"I do not need to earn my right to rest."* Inhale deeply. Exhale completely. Do this for one minute.

Mantra

My value is not in my output — it is in my being.

Evening Reflection

- Notice how your body responded today when you gave yourself permission to slow down. Guilt? Peace? Resistance?

_____
_____
_____
_____
_____
_____
_____

Day 135: Rest is Not Laziness

You were conditioned to feel guilty when you pause. To equate rest with weakness, and stillness with shame.

But rest is not laziness.
It's a return. A repair. A remembering.

Your body is not betraying you when it slows down. It's speaking the language of preservation.

Listen.
And let yourself be held by ease.

Morning Reflection

Many of us were taught that rest equals laziness. But rest is restoration. It is necessary for clarity, creativity, and healing.

Prompt

- **What childhood or cultural beliefs do you carry about rest?**

_____
_____
_____
_____
_____
_____
_____
_____

Mindful Minute

Lie down, place your hand over your heart, and whisper:

"I give myself permission to pause."

Mantra

Rest is a radical act of self-respect.

Evening Reflection

- **When did you resist rest today?**

_____
_____
_____
_____
_____
_____
_____
_____

- **What would it have looked like to allow it?**

_____
_____
_____
_____
_____
_____
_____
_____

Day 136 – Relearning the Language of Slow

You've spoken the dialect of urgency for so
long that silence feels loud,
and stillness feels wrong.

But there is a quieter rhythm waiting for
you— a pace that honors breath,
a tempo that lets you feel.

Relearning slow isn't
failure. It's fluency in
peace.
A reclamation of your nervous
system. A reunion with life,
unhurried.

Morning Reflection

Slowness invites presence. What could be different if
you stopped rushing and started noticing?

Prompt

- **List five areas of your life where slowness could be a gift.**

_____
_____
_____
_____
_____
_____
_____
_____

Mindful Minute

Eat or drink something slowly today. Fully taste it. No phone, no rush — just be.

Mantra

I slow down to meet myself.

Evening Reflection

- **What did you discover by moving slower today?**

_____
_____
_____
_____
_____
_____
_____
_____

Day 137 – The Nervous System Doesn't Lie

Long before your mind catches
on, your body already knows.

It flinches at fake safety.
It tenses around unmet
needs. It softens in truth.

You've been taught to ignore its signals—
to override the tremble, the tightness, the
tired. But your nervous system isn't
overreacting.
It's revealing.
It's remembering.
It's protecting.

Listen to it.
It never
lies.

Morning Reflection

- When we override exhaustion, we betray the signals our body is sending us. Your body always speaks first — were you listening?

Prompt

- What are three signs that your body gives when it needs rest?

Mindful Minute

- With each breath, scan your body from head to toe. Where are you tense? Breathe gently into those spaces.

_____
_____
_____
_____
_____
_____
_____
_____

Mantra

I trust my body's wisdom.

Evening Reflection

- **How did your body feel throughout the day?**

_____
_____
_____
_____
_____
_____
_____
_____

- **Did you honor its needs?**

_____
_____
_____
_____
_____
_____
_____
_____

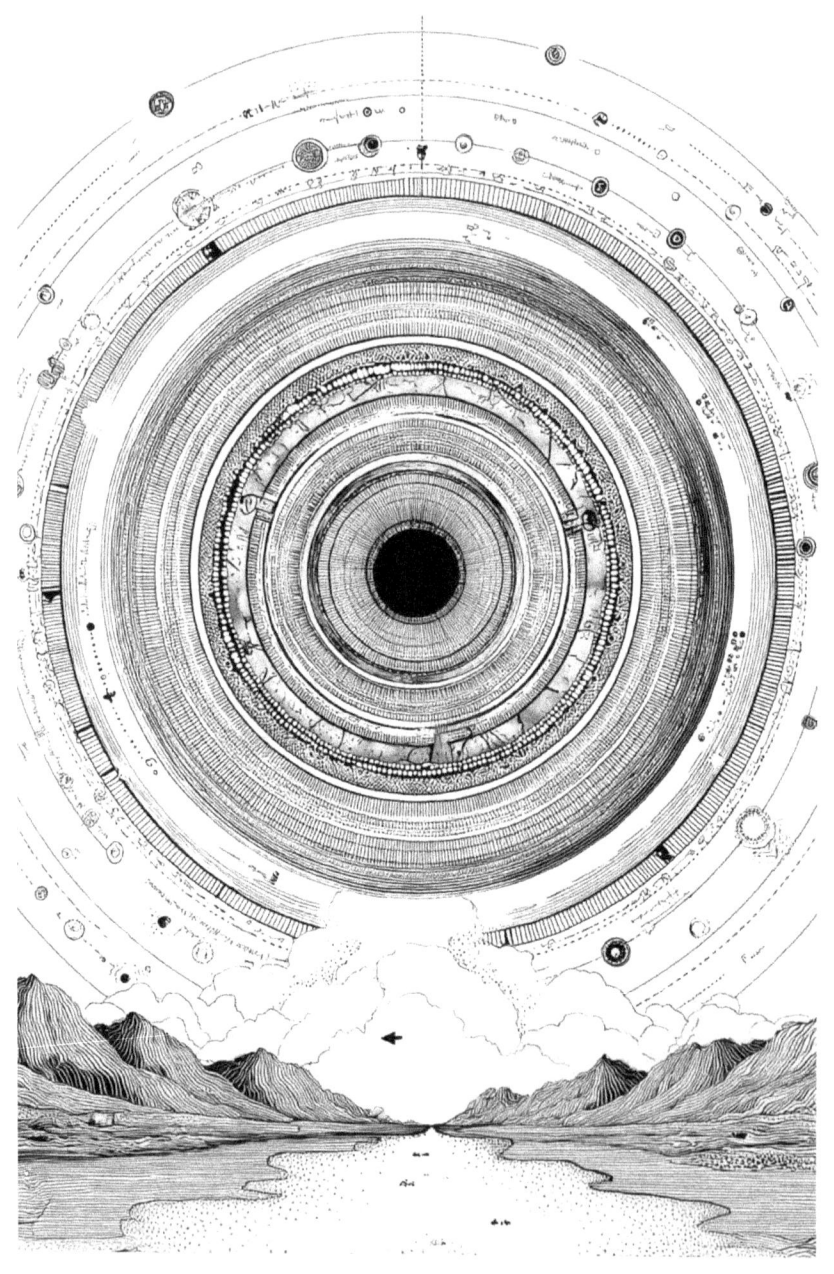

Day 138 – Guilt Around Doing 'Nothing'

Somewhere along the line, rest became a crime. Doing "nothing" started to feel like failing.

But doing nothing is not nothing. It is recovery.
It is rebellion against a world that worships exhaustion. It is presence without pressure.

You do not need to justify rest. You do not need to earn it.

Breathe.

Morning Reflection

Doing "nothing" is often when the most meaningful somethings surface. What are you afraid of finding in stillness?

Prompt

- **Write about a time you felt guilty for resting — and what you needed instead.**

_____
_____
_____
_____
_____
_____
_____
_____

Mindful Minute

Sit with your hands open in your lap. Repeat: *"I am enough, even when I am still."*

Mantra

I do not need to perform to be valuable.

Evening Reflection

- **Did guilt try to sneak into your rest today?**

_____
_____
_____
_____
_____
_____
_____

- **What did you tell it?**

Day 139 – The Power of an Unproductive Day

Not every day has to be about output.
Some days are simply meant for breathing, noticing, and being.

There is quiet power in days without checklists — days when you choose presence over performance, silence over striving.

You're not wasting
time. You're
reclaiming it.

Let these days remind you:
you are more than what you do.

Morning Reflection

Not every day needs to be optimized. Some days are for wandering, wondering, or simply existing.

Prompt

- **What would an intentionally "unproductive" day look like for you?**

_____
_____
_____
_____
_____
_____
_____
_____

Mindful Minute

Light a candle or sit near a window. Simply observe your environment. Let it ground you.

Mantra

Today, I choose presence over pressure.

Evening Reflection

- **What did your nervous system experience without the demand to perform?**

_____
_____
_____
_____
_____
_____
_____
_____

Day 140: Rest is Sacred

Rest isn't a reward — it's a right.
It's where your soul exhales, where your body remembers it's safe.

In a world that worships hustle, choosing rest is an act of defiance —
a quiet rebellion that says,
"I am already enough."

Let rest be more than
recovery. Let it be a ritual.
A return.
A reverence.

Morning Reflection

Rest is where the soul integrates. It is where healing catches up. Today, let your rest be sacred, not stolen.

Prompt

- **How can you design your week to include sacred rest — not leftovers?**

_____
_____
_____
_____
_____
_____
_____
_____

Mindful Minute

Lay flat, close your eyes, and whisper this blessing: *"I am held. I am safe. I can rest."*

Mantra

Sacred rest is my birthright.

Evening Reflection

- How did it feel to prioritize rest today — not as an afterthought, but as a necessity?

_____
_____
_____
_____
_____
_____
_____
_____

Week 21: "The Quiet Work of Healing"

Healing doesn't always announce itself. Sometimes it arrives in the quiet — when you let go of needing to be fixed and instead give yourself space to breathe, feel, and exist without judgment. This week honors the silent work your heart has been doing all along.

Day 141: Healing Without Headlines

Not every healing moment makes a grand entrance. Sometimes it's in the ordinary —
choosing a kind word over
silence, stepping outside for
fresh air, declining an invitation
without guilt.

Healing isn't always dramatic.
It doesn't need applause or
permission. It's quiet. Steady.
Yours.

And the world may never notice
— but you will.
And that's enough.

Morning Reflection:

You don't need to prove your healing to anyone. There's strength in growing quietly, far from the applause.

Prompt:

- **Where have I made quiet progress that I haven't acknowledged?**

_____
_____
_____
_____
_____
_____
_____
_____

Mindful Minute:

Place your palm over your chest. Breathe deeply into that space and thank your heart for all it's carried.

Mantra:

My growth is valid, even when it goes unseen.

Evening Reflection:

I noticed strength in the stillness today. I am softening, and that is enough.

Day 142: The Work Behind the Smile

There's a story behind your smile
— one that's been shaped by
endurance, disappointments
carried quietly,
and emotions held in until they faded.

You've shown up for others even
when you barely had anything left for
yourself. And that smile?
It's not fake. It's practiced. Earned.

Honor the work it took to wear
it. And don't forget —
you deserve to smile from a place of peace, too.

Morning Reflection:

- **Sometimes the brightest smile is covering the deepest work. What lies behind yours?**

_____
_____
_____
_____
_____
_____
_____
_____

Prompt:

- **What emotion am I currently carrying that I've been hiding?**

_____
_____
_____
_____
_____
_____
_____

Mindful Minute:

Sit with the part of yourself that feels heavy. No fixing — just noticing.

Mantra:

I don't have to smile to be okay.

Evening Reflection:

I honored my truth today. My smile belongs to no one but me.

Day 143: Invisible Milestones

Not every victory comes with applause.
Some look like getting out of bed when you didn't want to. Some are setting boundaries no one else understands.
Some are crying and letting it count as strength.

These are the milestones no one
sees. But you do.
And they matter.
Because healing isn't always loud —
sometimes, it's simply choosing yourself
again.

Morning Reflection:

Not every milestone is loud. Sometimes it's waking up with a little more hope. Sometimes, it's not reacting the way you used to.

Prompt:

- **What invisible victory did I achieve this week?**

_____
_____
_____
_____
_____
_____
_____
_____

Mindful Minute:

Breathe and remember a moment this week when you chose differently. Feel that growth.

Mantra:

My evolution is mine to celebrate.

Evening Reflection:

Today I remembered that I've come further than I give myself credit for.

Day 144: Breaking Generational Echoes

There are patterns passed down not through
intention, but through survival —
the silence, the shutdowns, the shame.

You may not have asked for
them, but you carry the power to
end them.

Every time you respond instead of
react, express instead of suppress,
hold instead of harm —
you break an echo that's long been sounding.

That's not
rebellion. That's
healing.

Morning Reflection:

You weren't born with the wounds you carry. Some were passed down. But healing can start — and stop — with you.

Prompt:

- **What inherited belief about masculinity no longer serves me?**

_____
_____
_____
_____
_____
_____
_____
_____

Mindful Minute:

Gently say aloud: "This ends with me." Let it echo in your body.

Mantra:

I am not my father's pain.

Evening Reflection:

Today I honored the courage it takes to be different — and to heal for those who never could.

Day 145: Healing Without a Finish Line

Healing is not a race with medals or applause. There's no finish line, no grand ceremony.

It's the quiet choosing
— to show up again,
to tend to what still hurts,
to meet yourself with honesty instead of haste.

Some days it feels like progress,
other days like starting over.
Both are valid.

Healing isn't about arriving.
It's about becoming — again and again.

Morning Reflection:

Healing isn't a race. It's not linear. There's no final medal
— only layers and more softness.

Prompt:

- **Where am I still holding on to a timeline for my healing?**

_____
_____
_____
_____
_____
_____
_____
_____

Mindful Minute:

Close your eyes. Imagine your healing as a spiral, not a straight line. Allow yourself to be where you are.

Mantra:

I release the pressure to be done.

Evening Reflection:

I gave myself grace today. I am healing at my own pace.

Day 146: Permission to Be Tender

You don't need to earn the right to be gentle.
Not with others — and certainly not with
yourself.

Tenderness is not a detour from
strength. It *is* strength.
The kind that stays soft in a hard world.
The kind that offers comfort when there's nothing
left to fix.

You are allowed to be
tender. With your
thoughts.
With your fears.
With the parts of you still

healing. Let tenderness guide

you home.

Morning Reflection:

Being tender doesn't make you less of a man — it
makes you more human.

Prompt:

- **Where in my life am I craving tenderness, but too afraid to ask for it?**

_____
_____
_____
_____
_____
_____
_____
_____

Mindful Minute:

Wrap your arms around yourself and hold for one full breath cycle. This is your tenderness.

Mantra:

I deserve to feel safe in softness.

Evening Reflection:

I leaned into tenderness today. I am learning to receive.

Day 147: The Day Nothing Hurts

Some days, the ache goes quiet.
The thoughts don't race. The weight feels lighter.
And for a moment — maybe longer — you breathe
without bracing.

This is not forgetting the pain.
It's remembering that healing is
possible. That you're allowed joy
without guilt.

Let this be a soft
reminder: Not every day
will hurt.
And that in itself... is a kind of miracle.

Morning Reflection:

Some days arrive quietly, and nothing aches. Those days are sacred. Receive them without suspicion.

Prompt:

- **What would it feel like to let myself fully enjoy peace when it comes?**

_____
_____
_____
_____
_____
_____
_____
_____

Mindful Minute:

Let your shoulders drop. Let your jaw unclench. Let the peace stay longer.

Mantra:

It's okay to feel good.

Evening Reflection:

I allowed joy today. I didn't wait for it to be taken.

Week 22: "Rest Is Not Retreat"

This week is about redefining rest as a form of resistance, not laziness. You weren't made to be productive every minute. You were made to feel, breathe, and be. Rest is a sacred pause, not a sign of weakness.

Day 148: Rest Without Guilt

Rest is not something you have to earn.
Not a reward. Not a break between doing

more. It's a right — yours.

You don't need to apologize for catching your breath, for slowing your pace,
for simply being.

Guilt may whisper, but it doesn't speak truth.
Because choosing
rest is choosing life.

Morning Reflection:

You don't have to earn your rest. It is your right, not a reward.

Prompt:

- **Where in my life do I tie my worth to how hard I push myself?**

_____
_____
_____
_____
_____
_____
_____
_____

Mindful Minute:

Breathe in the word "enough." Breathe out the word "guilt." Repeat.

Mantra:

My rest is as important as my work.

Evening Reflection:

Today I honored my body's need to slow down —
without apology.

Day 149: The Pause That Saves

Sometimes, all it takes is one

pause. One breath before the

spiral.
One moment before the
reaction. One heartbeat before
the shutdown.

That pause isn't weakness — it's wisdom.
It's your nervous system saying: *Wait. I need a second.*
It's your healing speaking up.

The pause doesn't delay your
progress. It protects it.

Morning Reflection:

Sometimes the most powerful thing you can do is stop before you break.

Prompt:

- **What signs of burnout have I ignored lately?**

_____
_____
_____
_____
_____
_____
_____
_____

Mindful Minute:

Place one hand on your chest and the other on your stomach. Feel the rise and fall. This is your body saying "stay."

Mantra:

Pausing is not quitting.

Evening Reflection:

I paused when I needed to today. I chose myself.

Day 150: Sacred Laziness

What if laziness isn't a flaw — but a flag?
A signal that your body and mind need a break.

You weren't made to grind without grace.
You were made to live, to breathe, to be.

Sacred laziness is choosing stillness without shame. It's resting without apology.
It's trusting that your worth was never tied to how much you do.

Morning Reflection:

Call it sacred. Call it essential. But stop calling your rest "lazy."

Prompt:

- **When was the last time I truly did nothing — and how did it feel?**

_____
_____
_____
_____
_____
_____
_____
_____

Mindful Minute:

Sit in silence for one full minute with no goal but to be here.

Mantra:

Doing nothing is sometimes doing everything I need.

Evening Reflection:

Today I made room for stillness. I felt no need to explain it.

Month 5 Reflection: Growth Checkpoint

1. **How I've Changed Since Day 1**

- **Mentally rewind to where you started. What's noticeably shifted?**

_____
_____
_____
_____
_____
_____
_____

Day 151: Rest as Rebellion

In a world that praises burnout and busyness, choosing rest is a quiet revolution.

It's saying no to proving.
No to pleasing.
No to productivity as identity.

Rest becomes a way of reclaiming
yourself— your rhythm, your breath,
your being.

Not laziness.
But
liberation.

Morning Reflection:

In a world that profits from your exhaustion, rest becomes a radical act.

Prompt:

- **What part of me resists rest the most — and why?**

_____
_____
_____
_____
_____
_____
_____
_____

Mindful Minute:

With every breath, imagine setting down a heavy weight you've been carrying too long.

Mantra:

I rest, and in doing so, I resist.

Evening Reflection:

I rested today not because I'm weak, but because I am wise.

Day 152: The Fear of Falling Behind

It lingers in your chest—
the anxiety that if you pause, you'll lose
ground. That while you rest, others are racing
ahead.

But healing doesn't happen at full
speed. And wholeness doesn't
compete.

You are not
behind. You are
becoming— at
your own pace,
on your own terms.

Morning Reflection:

The fear of being left behind will rob you of the
present.
You are not late. You are living.

Prompt:

- **Where do I feel behind in life, and what might it mean to release that belief?**

_____
_____
_____
_____
_____
_____
_____
_____

Mindful Minute:

Say to yourself: "I am not behind. I am becoming."
Feel that truth settle in.

Mantra:

My pace is perfect for my path.

Evening Reflection:

I gave myself permission to exist outside the clock today.

Day 153: The Body Remembers

Long after your mind forgets,
your body still holds the
echoes— of raised voices,
of unmet needs,
of tension you had no name for.

Healing begins with
listening. To the tight
shoulders,
the shallow breath,
the fatigue that lingers.

Your body is not betraying
you. It's trying to tell you

Morning Reflection:

Your body keeps the score — not just of pain, but also of peace. Give it new memories.

Prompt:

- **How has my body been asking for gentleness lately?**

_____
_____
_____
_____
_____
_____
_____
_____

Mindful Minute:

Stretch gently. Scan your body. Thank each part for carrying you.

Mantra:

I treat my body like someone I love.

Evening Reflection:

Today I listened to my body instead of overriding it. I offered peace.

Day 154: The Permission Slip

You don't have to wait
for someone else to say you're allowed.

You can write your own permission
slip— to rest,
to grieve,
to want more,
to stop performing.

Your healing doesn't need an
audience. Your softness doesn't
need validation.

You are allowed
because you are
human.

Morning Reflection:

If you're waiting for permission to rest, let this be it.
You don't need to break to be worthy of recovery.

Prompt:

- What kind of rest would nourish me the most right now — mental, emotional, physical, or spiritual?

Mindful Minute:

- Write yourself a literal permission slip to rest. Read it aloud.

Mantra:

I give myself full permission to slow down.

Evening Reflection:

I accepted the gift of rest today. It felt like a homecoming.

Week 23: "Grounding Through Nature"

This week reconnects you with the Earth — the original place of stillness, safety, and truth. Nature doesn't rush, yet everything is accomplished. There's healing in the soil, in the air, in simply being.

Day 155: Earth Beneath Me

When the world feels
unsteady, return to what
holds you.

The earth beneath your feet
doesn't demand your
performance. It only asks you
to arrive.
To breathe.
To remember that you're supported.

You don't have to hold
everything. Let the ground carry
some of it.

Morning Reflection:

Let the ground remind you: you are supported, always.

Prompt:

- What does it mean for me to be "grounded"?

_____
_____
_____
_____
_____
_____
_____
_____

- **What takes me away from that feeling?**

_____
_____
_____
_____
_____
_____
_____
_____

Mindful Minute:

Stand barefoot if possible. Feel each toe, each root, connect you to something ancient.

Mantra:

I am held by the Earth beneath me.

Evening Reflection:

Today I remembered that I do not walk this world alone.
The ground carries me.

Day 156: My Place in the Wild

Morning Reflection:

You are not apart from nature. You are a part of it.

Prompt:

- **When was the last time I felt truly alive in the natural world?**

_____
_____
_____
_____
_____
_____
_____
_____

Mindful Minute:

Visualize a peaceful natural setting — forest, ocean, desert, or mountain. Breathe as though you're there.

Mantra:

I am a living part of nature's rhythm.

Evening Reflection:

I honored my connection to nature today — even if only by breathing with intention.

Day 157: Sky Above, Peace Within

Look up.
The sky reminds you: you're part of something vast, something that doesn't rush,
doesn't
strive— just is.

Let it soften you.
Let it remind you that peace isn't found in control, but in surrender.

You, too, can stretch
wide, and still be held.

Morning Reflection:

The sky doesn't ask you to perform. It simply exists — vast, open, and free. So can you.

Prompt:

- **What would I let go of if I believed I was already enough?**

_____
_____
_____
_____
_____
_____
_____
_____

Mindful Minute:

Look up at the sky today — even just for a moment.
Let your breath match its vastness.

Mantra:

There is peace above and peace within.

Evening Reflection:

Under the same sky as everyone else, I felt a moment of belonging.

Day 158: The Healing Wind

Let the wind pass through
you— not just over your skin,
but through the places you've kept shut too long.

It doesn't need to fix
anything. Just remind you
to breathe.
To feel.
To remember that even unseen things—like
wind—can carry healing.

Not all healing arrives with noise.
Some come like a breeze: quiet, constant, and
kind.

Morning Reflection:

The wind doesn't ask for permission to move. Let it
teach you freedom.

Prompt:

- **What do I wish I could release today, as freely as the wind?**

_____
_____
_____
_____
_____
_____
_____
_____

Mindful Minute:

Stand outdoors. Feel the breeze on your skin. Let it carry your tension away.

Mantra:

I am allowed to let go.

Evening Reflection:

I felt the wind today — and I remembered how to release without regret.

Day 159: My Nervous System in Nature

Out here, the body remembers.

The rhythm of leaves, the patience of

trees, the grounding of bare feet on

earth—

they all speak a language my nervous system understands.

In nature, I don't have to

perform. I just have to be.

And in being, I begin to

regulate. To settle.

To return.

Morning Reflection:

Your nervous system finds safety in trees, rivers, birdsong.
Nature regulates what chaos disrupts.

Prompt:

- **What natural setting makes me feel safest?**

_____
_____
_____
_____
_____
_____
_____

- **How can I visit it — physically or mentally — more often?**

_____
_____
_____
_____
_____
_____
_____

Mindful Minute:

Breathe in slowly while imagining the scent of fresh rain or forest air.

Mantra:

Nature is my medicine.

Evening Reflection:

My body softened today — not because I forced it, but because I returned to what's natural.

Day 160: Fire and Softness

There's a fire in me —
not the kind that burns everything
down, but the kind that keeps me
warm.

Strength doesn't have to
roar. Sometimes it glows.
Softness doesn't mean the fire is
gone. It means it's safe now.
Safe enough to be
kind. To be gentle.
To be whole.

Morning Reflection:

There's fire in you — and softness, too. The sun warms
and doesn't burn. So can you.

Prompt:

- **Where in my life do I confuse force with strength?**

_____
_____
_____
_____
_____
_____
_____
_____

Mindful Minute:

Feel the warmth of sunlight on your skin today — even just through a window. Let it soften you.

Mantra:

I carry strength without hardness.

Evening Reflection:

The fire in me did not consume me today — it comforted me.

Day 161: A Quiet Place Within

Amid the noise of obligation, expectation, and survival, there lives a quieter place inside you — one untouched by performance or pressure.

You don't have to escape to find peace. You can return to it.
Because peace isn't always found.
Sometimes, it's remembered.

Morning Reflection:

Just like the hush in a forest or a still lake at dawn — you have quiet places within you.

Prompt:

- **What does internal stillness feel like to me? When was the last time I touched it?**

_____
_____
_____
_____
_____
_____
_____

Mindful Minute:

Close your eyes.

Listen only to your breath.

No fixing.

Just

listening.

Mantra:

I am allowed to be still.

Evening Reflection:

Today, I found peace in stillness — not because I escaped the world, but because I returned to myself.

Week 24: "Let That Sh*t Go: Perfectionism"

This week, we make peace with imperfection. You don't have to earn love by being flawless. You are enough — flawed, healing, growing, human. Let go of the pressure. Let in the truth.

Day 162: The Myth of Being Enough

You've been told to strive to *be enough* —
as if your worth could ever be measured or earned.

But "enough" is a moving target.
A myth rooted in scarcity and comparison.

You are not here to prove.
You are here to live, to feel, to be.
You were always worthy — before the striving began.

Morning Reflection:

There's no finish line where you suddenly become "worthy." You already are.

Prompt:

- **What do I believe I must achieve before I am enough?**

_____
_____
_____
_____
_____
_____
_____

Mindful Minute:

Place your hand on your chest.

Repeat: "I am enough, even now."

Mantra:

I am not a project — I am a person.

Evening Reflection:

Today I reminded myself that healing doesn't require perfection.

Day 163: Permission to Mess Up

You will get it wrong sometimes.
You will stumble, say the wrong thing, choose the harder path.

But healing isn't perfection — it's movement. And growth rarely looks graceful.

You're allowed to mess up.
What matters is returning — to yourself, to truth, to intention.
That's where the power lives.

Morning Reflection:

Mistakes don't disqualify you from love — they make you human.

Prompt:

- What "mistake" am I still punishing myself for?

_____
_____
_____
_____
_____
_____
_____
_____

Mindful Minute:

Inhale forgiveness. Exhale shame. Visualize letting it go.

Mantra:

I release the need to be flawless.

Evening Reflection:

I gave myself permission to be human — and it felt like peace.

Day 164: The Weight of Control

Control often feels like safety —
a way to quiet the chaos, protect from pain,
prevent the unknown.

But the more you grip, the heavier it becomes.
Control asks you to tighten your shoulders, predict
every outcome, brace for every fall.
It leaves no room for trust. No space for grace.

The truth is, some things are meant to flow, not be
fixed. Some days are meant to unfold, not be
managed.

Letting go isn't weakness —
it's choosing freedom over
fear.

Morning Reflection:

Perfectionism is often fear in disguise — fear of being
seen, being judged, or being not enough.

Prompt:

- **Where am I trying to control things that are out of my hands?**

_____
_____
_____
_____
_____
_____
_____
_____

Mindful Minute:

Loosen your fists. Physically relax your shoulders.
Name what you can't control — then let it be.

Mantra:

I surrender what isn't mine to hold.

Evening Reflection:

Today I practiced softening my grip — and I survived the letting go.

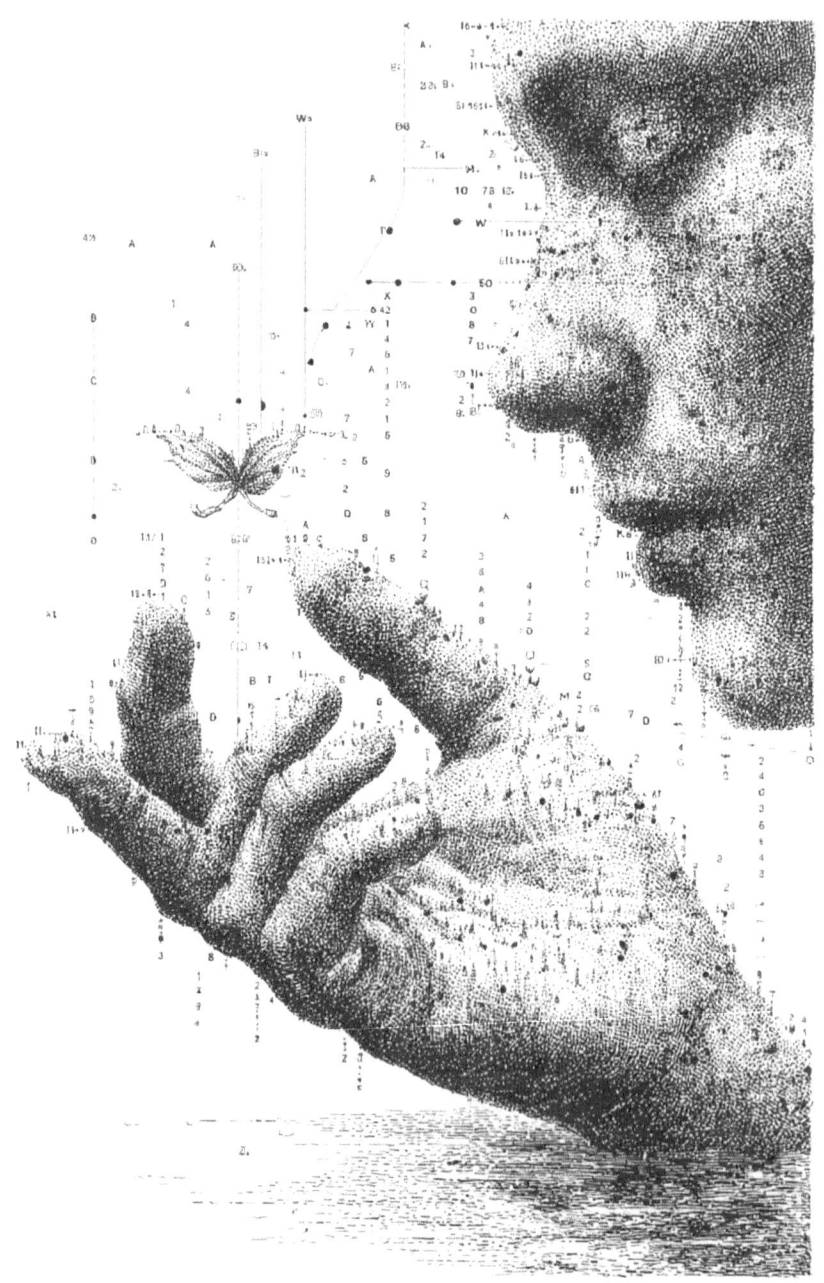

Day 165: Flaws Are Part of the Story

You've been taught to tidy yourself up —
to edit, to perform, to hide the parts that don't shine.

But your flaws are not failures.
They are fingerprints of your becoming.
Proof that you've lived, tried, stretched,
broken, and healed.

The cracks in your story let the
humanity in. And that is where
connection lives —
not in perfection, but in the truth of being
whole and unfinished.

Morning Reflection:

Your cracks are where your light gets in — and where your truth comes out.

Prompt:

- **What flaw have I tried to hide that actually makes me more relatable or human?**

_____
_____
_____
_____
_____
_____
_____

Mindful Minute:

Look in the mirror and say, "This version of me is worthy, too."

Mantra:

I am whole, not because I'm perfect — but because I'm real.

Evening Reflection:

I chose to show up today as I am — not as a curated version.

Day 166: The Productivity Trap

You learned to measure your worth by output —
how much you do, how fast you move, how useful you are.

But constantly producing is not the same as
living. You are more than your checklists.
More than your calendar.
More than what you get done in a day.

Freedom begins when you stop
proving, and start *being*.
You are enough — even when you rest.

Morning Reflection:

You are not what you produce. You are not your output.

Prompt:

- Where am I tying my worth to how much I do?

_____
_____
_____
_____
_____
_____
_____
_____

Mindful Minute:

Sit with one deep breath per finger — 10 breaths, slow and present.

Mantra:

My value is not measured in checklists.

Evening Reflection:

I slowed down today — and I was still worthy.

Day 167: Good Enough Is Enough

You've spent years chasing perfection —
believing that if you could just do it
flawlessly, they would stay, love, approve,
applaud.

But perfection is a prison.
And "good enough" isn't settling
— it's freedom.

There's power in doing your
best and letting it *be* enough.
You are not failing.
You're learning to breathe outside the
performance.

Morning Reflection:

"Perfect" is the enemy of progress. "Good enough" is a revolution.

Prompt:

- What would I start — or finish — if I didn't need it to be perfect?

_____
_____
_____
_____
_____
_____
_____
_____

Mindful Minute:

Take one imperfect action today. Breathe through the discomfort.

Mantra:

Done is better than perfect.

Evening Reflection:

I chose progress over perfection — and that was powerful.

Day 168: I Am Already Becoming

Growth isn't always loud.
It doesn't always come with applause or big moments. Sometimes, it's in the quiet choices—
the deep breaths, the honest no, the softer inner voice.

You're not
behind. You're
not lost.

You are already becoming—
even when it doesn't feel like
it. Trust the unfolding.

Morning Reflection:

There's no version of you that's "finally lovable." That version is already here.

Prompt:

- **What part of me have I been withholding until I feel "ready"?**

_____
_____
_____
_____
_____
_____
_____

Mindful Minute:

Breathe in acceptance. Picture yourself unfolding gently, just as you are.

Mantra:

I am not behind. I am on time for my own life.

Evening Reflection:

I stopped rushing toward a future version of me — and welcomed the man I already am.

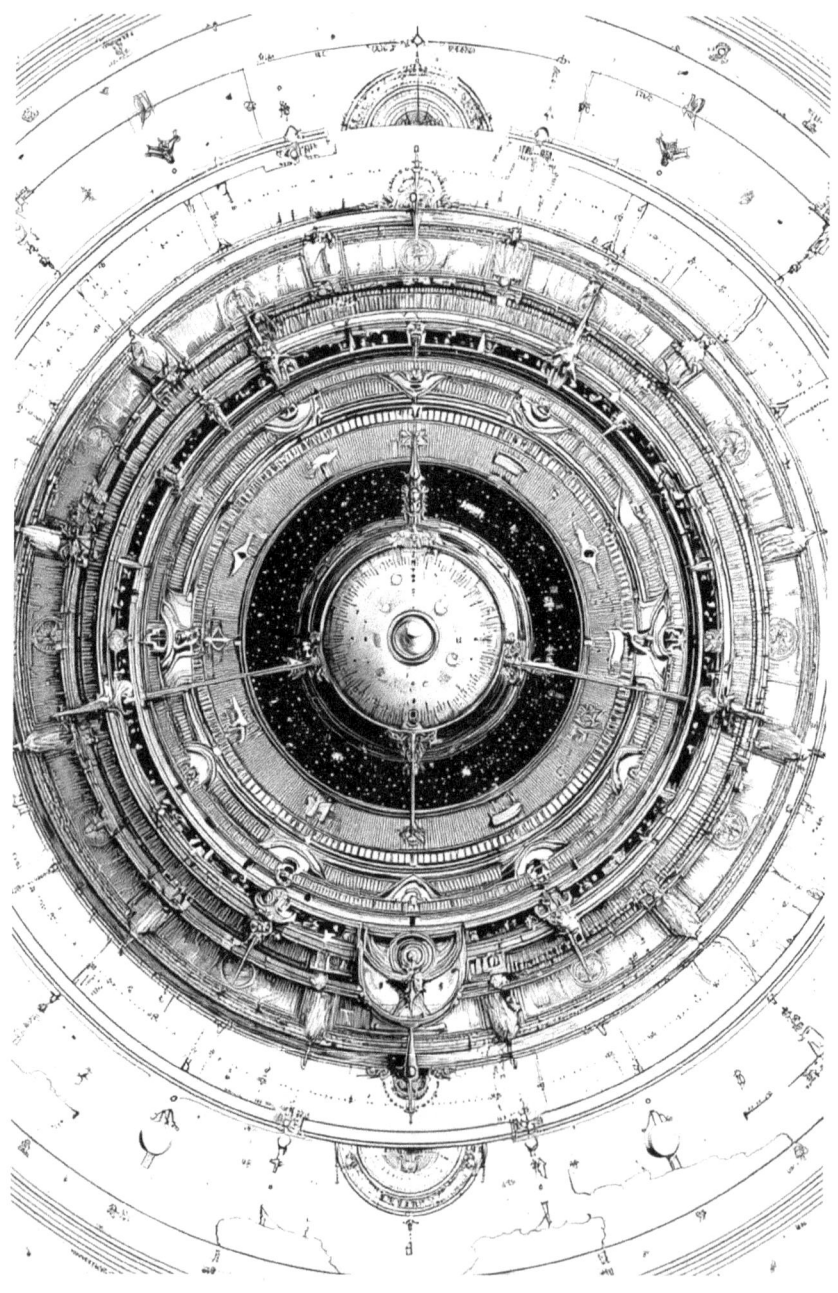

Week 25: Reclaiming Emotional Intimacy

This week is about letting others truly *see* you. Vulnerability is not weakness — it's the raw material of real connection. You've armored up long enough. Now, you learn how to let love in.

Day 169: Seen, Not Just Strong

Being strong got you through a lot.
But strength without being seen can turn into silence. You deserve more than admiration for your resilience— you deserve to be witnessed in your fullness.

Not just as the one who holds everything together, but as someone with softness, needs, and a story.

It's not too much to want to be
seen. It's human.

Morning Reflection:

Strength without visibility becomes isolation. Who sees you beyond what you do?

Prompt:

- **What do I wish others truly knew or understood about me?**

_____
_____
_____
_____
_____
_____
_____
_____

Mindful Minute:

Place a hand on your heart and say:

"I want to be seen. I deserve to be seen."

Mantra:

I am worthy of being seen, not just relied upon.

Evening Reflection:

I gave myself permission to be visible in ways that mattered today.

Day 170: The Courage to Be Known

It takes strength to carry pain alone.
But it takes even more courage to let someone in.

To be known—not for what you do,
but for who you are beneath the
armor.

Letting yourself be seen in your joy, your
fears, your questions, and your hopes
isn't weakness.
It's the kind of bravery that heals.

Morning Reflection:

People can't love a mask — only the man underneath.

Prompt:

- **What parts of myself do I hide, even from people I trust?**

_____
_____
_____
_____
_____
_____
_____
_____

Mindful Minute:

Breathe into your belly. Whisper: "I don't have to hide here."

Mantra:

The real me deserves real connection.

Evening Reflection:

I honored my truth today — and it didn't destroy me.

Day 171: The Cost of Withholding

We learned to withhold—
our feelings, our stories, our
tears— believing silence kept us
safe.

But what we don't
say doesn't
disappear.
It sits quietly,
heavy in our
chest, waiting to
be felt.

The cost of withholding isn't just disconnection
from others.
It's the slow forgetting of our own truth.

Morning Reflection:

When you withhold your truth, your
relationships stay surface-level — and so does
your peace.

Prompt:

- **What am I afraid will happen if I speak my truth to someone I love?**

_____
_____
_____
_____
_____
_____
_____
_____

Mindful Minute:

Breathe in gently. Exhale slowly. Imagine your words landing softly, not destructively.

Mantra:

I release fear around my truth.

Evening Reflection:

I considered the weight of what I don't say — and how much it costs me.

Day 172: Let Love In

You've learned how to protect
yourself— walls high, doors locked,
heart guarded.

But protection isn't the same as
peace. And safety without love is still
loneliness.

Letting love in isn't weakness.
It's choosing to believe that being
known is worth the risk.
That your softness deserves holding too.

Morning Reflection:

It's not just about giving love — it's about learning
how to let it in.

Prompt:

- **When was the last time I fully received care, affection, or love?**

_____
_____
_____
_____
_____
_____
_____
_____

Mindful Minute:

Visualize a moment where you were loved. Let it sink in.
Let it stay.

Mantra:

I am open to love. I am safe with love.

Evening Reflection:

I allowed myself to receive today — and I didn't shrink from it.

Day 173: Vulnerability Is Strength

You were taught to hide what hurt, to mask emotion, to "man up."

But real strength isn't in silence— it's in truth-telling.

Vulnerability is not collapse. It's courage in motion.
It's standing with your heart open and saying,
"This is me—and I'm still here."

Morning Reflection:

To open up when it's easier to shut down — that's strength.

Prompt:

- **What conversation have I been avoiding because it feels too raw?**

_____
_____
_____
_____
_____
_____
_____
_____

Mindful Minute:

Repeat: "I can be soft without being small."

Mantra:

My softness is my strength.

Evening Reflection:

I showed up today with a little less armor — and more heart.

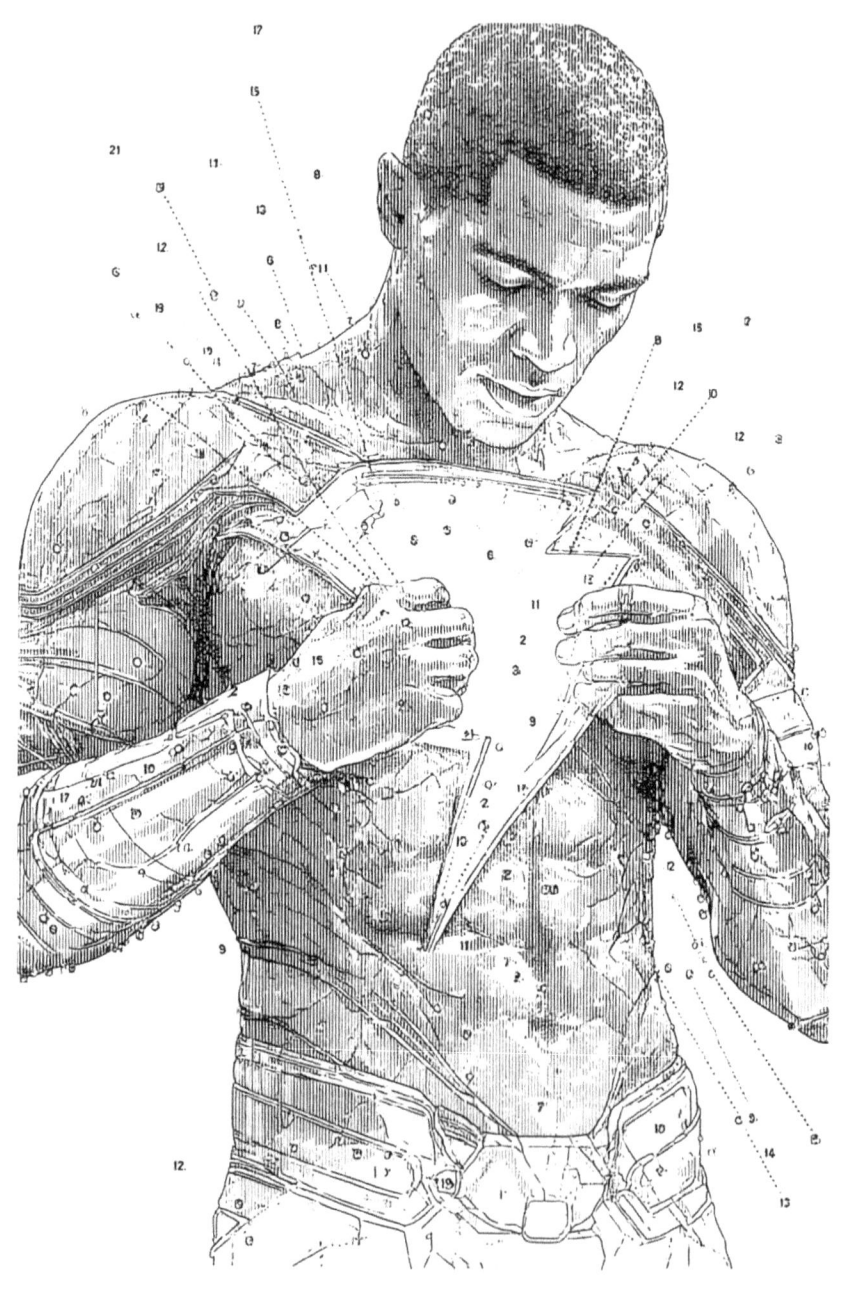

Day 174: Intimacy Requires Integrity

Real closeness isn't built on charm or control.
It's born from the quiet, consistent
choice to show up honestly.

To be known,
you must let yourself be
seen— not just the polished
parts,
but the tender truths too.

Intimacy asks for
truthfulness, not
perfection.
For presence, not performance.
It requires the courage
to bring your whole self to the table.

Morning Reflection:

You can't build closeness on silence or pretense. You have to show up in truth.

Prompt:

- **Have I ever stayed silent just to "keep the peace"? What did it cost me?**

_____
_____
_____
_____
_____
_____
_____
_____

Mindful Minute:

Sit in stillness. Let your breath remind you that truth is safe.

Mantra:

My truth builds bridges, not walls.

Evening Reflection:

Today I honored both my truth and my relationships — even when it felt vulnerable.

Day 175: Emotional Intimacy Begins With Me

Before I can be fully known by
another, I must first learn to stay
with myself— to notice what I feel,
to name it without shame,
to meet my own heart without flinching.

Emotional intimacy isn't just
shared— it's built inside.

It's the sacred practice of not abandoning
myself, even when it would be easier to go
numb.

Morning Reflection:

If you can't be emotionally honest with yourself, you can't be emotionally available to others.

Prompt:

- Where am I emotionally unavailable — to myself or others?

_____
_____
_____
_____
_____
_____
_____
_____

Mindful Minute:

Place one hand on your chest and one on your belly.

Breathe deeply. Say, "I am here. I am listening."

Mantra:

I meet myself with honesty and care.

Evening Reflection:

I connected with my emotional self today — and it made space for deeper connection with others.

Week 26: Unlearning The Hustle Trap

You were never meant to walk this road alone. This week is about rediscovering the power of brotherhood — the kind that holds space, speaks truth, and doesn't flinch at your tears.

Day 176: Remembering Brotherhood

There was a time when brotherhood meant laughter without armor,
competition without
cruelty, presence without
pressure.

Somewhere along the line,
we traded connection for
toughness— support for silence.

But we were never meant to journey
alone. Brotherhood is not weakness.
It is
survival. It
is strength.
It is the soft place to land
when the world forgets your name.

Morning Reflection:

True brotherhood is not about competition — it's about belonging.

Prompt:

- **When in my life did I feel genuinely supported by male friendship?**

_____
_____
_____
_____
_____
_____
_____

Mindful Minute:

Visualize the face of a friend who's shown up for you. Let that memory ground you.

Mantra:

I am not alone in this journey.

Evening Reflection:

I remembered the strength that comes from being seen by another man today.

Day 177: Competitive by Default

Competition can be a fire that fuels growth—or a shadow that steals connection.
Too often, we fall into rivalry not by choice, but by default, measuring our worth against others instead of within ourselves.

But life isn't a race to outrun one another.
True strength lies in collaboration, in lifting each other up, and redefining success on our own terms.

Morning Reflection:

- **When did we learn to compete instead of connect?**

_____
_____
_____
_____
_____
_____
_____

Prompt:

- **Where in my life am I choosing competition over connection with other men?**

_____
_____
_____
_____
_____
_____
_____
_____

Mindful Minute:

Breathe into the word "enough." You don't need to prove anything here.

Mantra:

There's room for all of us to win.

Evening Reflection:

Today, I looked at another man and saw a brother — not a rival.

Day 178: Where Did All the Friends Go?

Friendship is a quiet refuge—sometimes it fades not because of distance,
but because life's burdens pull us away, piece by piece. We wonder where the laughter went, the late-night talks, the shared dreams.

Yet, friendships that endure are never truly lost; they live in memories and in the hope of new beginnings. To find them again, we must first find ourselves—ready to give and receive.

Morning Reflection:

Adulthood has a way of isolating us — but connection is still within reach.

Prompt:

- **What has kept me from maintaining deep male friendships?**

_____
_____
_____
_____
_____
_____
_____
_____

Mindful Minute:

Whisper to yourself: "I deserve connection."

Let it settle in your chest.

Mantra:

I will not abandon my need for connection.

Evening Reflection:

I reflected on friendships lost — and those still worth building.

Day 179: Emotional Fluency Among Men

Many of us were taught that silence is strength, that feelings are a foreign language spoken only in private. But emotional fluency isn't weakness—it's wisdom.

It's the ability to name what aches, to listen without fixing, to say "I'm hurting" without shame.

Among men, this fluency builds bridges— where isolation once stood, now there is belonging.

Morning Reflection:

We need more than jokes and surface talk. We need real conversations.

Prompt:

- **What emotional conversations have I longed to have with male friends?**

_____
_____
_____
_____
_____
_____
_____
_____

Mindful Minute:

Repeat three times: "It's okay to speak what I feel."

Mantra:

My emotions have a place in brotherhood.

Evening Reflection:

I honored my emotions today — and imagined sharing them with another man.

Day 180: Reaching Out

It's brave to ask for help.
To say, *"I can't do this alone."*
To reach, even with trembling hands.

You were never meant to carry it all in silence.
Connection doesn't make you needy—
it makes you human.

There is no shame in needing others.
There is strength in letting yourself be seen.

Morning Reflection:

- **Sometimes the first move toward healing is a message, a call, or a simple, "How are you, really?"**

_____
_____
_____
_____
_____
_____
_____

Prompt:

- **Who do I need to reconnect with — even if it's been a long time?**

_____
_____
_____
_____
_____
_____
_____
_____

Mindful Minute:

Visualize your hand reaching out. Imagine it being received.

Mantra:

I am allowed to reach out.

Evening Reflection:

I took a step toward connection today — and it mattered.

Day 181: Holding Space for Another Man

Sometimes the greatest gift you can
offer is simply your presence.
No fixing. No judging. No rushing.

Just being there—
shoulder to
shoulder, heart to
heart.

Because men need safe places,
too. Places to unravel.
Places to just be.
And sometimes, that place is you.

Morning Reflection:

Being strong for another doesn't mean fixing — it means being present.

Prompt:

- How can I show up better for my male friends — without judgment, solutions, or silence?

_____
_____
_____
_____
_____
_____
_____
_____

Mindful Minute:

Breathe in: "Presence."

Breathe out: "Compassion."

Mantra:

My presence is enough.

Evening Reflection:

I thought about how I can hold space, not just take it.

Month 6 Reflection: Mid-Year Mirror

1. **What I Want to Remember from This Journey**

- Capture a moment, thought, or insight that defines the last 6 months.

_____
_____
_____
_____
_____
_____
_____
_____
_____
_____
_____
_____

Day 182: Brotherhood as Sanctuary

True brotherhood isn't loud.
It doesn't always announce
itself. Sometimes it shows up
in silence, in consistency,
in knowing glances and honest words.

It's the place where you're not
measured, but met.
Not expected to
perform, but invited to
exhale.

Brotherhood, at its
best, becomes a
sanctuary— where
healing begins
simply because you are seen.

Morning Reflection:

- What if friendship among men could be a soft place to land?

Prompt:

- What would a healthy, emotionally safe brotherhood look like in my life?

Mindful Minute:

Imagine standing in a circle of men where no part of you is rejected.

Mantra:

I am building a circle where we all belong.

Evening Reflection:

I dreamed of sanctuary today — and remembered it begins with one honest connection.

Week 27: Expressing Without Fixing

Expression doesn't always need a solution. This week is about giving yourself and others permission to feel and share — without rushing to fix, correct, or minimize.

Day 183: You Don't Have to Fix It

Sometimes, presence is
enough. You don't have to
offer solutions.
You don't have to carry every burden.

Just being there — fully, quietly,
honestly — is its own kind of healing.
Let your love be a soft
place, not a tool.

You're not weak for not having
answers. You're human — and
sometimes,
that's exactly what someone needs most.

Morning Reflection:

You can be present without problem-solving.
Listening is its own form of love.

Prompt:

- **What's one area of my life I've tried to fix instead of feel?**

_____
_____
_____
_____
_____
_____
_____
_____
_____

Mindful Minute:

Place a hand on your chest and breathe. Say silently:
"I'm allowed to just be with it."

Mantra:

My presence is powerful, even in silence.

Evening Reflection:

I gave myself permission to feel without searching for answers today.

Day 184: When We Minimize Our Pain

We've learned to downplay what
hurts. To call it "not that deep."
To laugh it off.
To compare it to worse.

But pain doesn't need permission to be valid.
It doesn't have to reach a certain volume to
matter. Your wounds don't need a scoreboard.

What hurt you deserves your
attention — not dismissal.
Honoring your pain
is the first step toward healing it.

Morning Reflection:

Saying "it's nothing" doesn't make the pain go away. It just buries it deeper.

Prompt:

- **Where have I minimized my emotional pain to avoid discomfort?**

_____
_____
_____
_____
_____
_____
_____
_____

Mindful Minute:

Inhale: *"My pain is valid."*

Exhale: *"I do not have to hide it."*

Mantra:

I honor what hurts.

Evening Reflection:

Today I acknowledged pain I've long dismissed. That was brave.

Day 185: Let It Be Messy

Healing doesn't follow a script.
Some days are clear. Others,
confusing. There are tears without
reasons,
and peace that shows up unannounced.

Let it be messy.
Let the cracks breathe.
You're not doing it wrong
— you're just doing it
honestly.

This isn't about
perfection. It's about
presence.

Morning Reflection:

There is no perfect way to express emotion. Let it be clumsy, loud, raw — it's still real.

Prompt:

What stops me from expressing myself messily?

_____
_____
_____
_____
_____
_____
_____
_____

Mindful Minute:

Shake your arms out. Loosen the body. Let go of needing it to be neat.

Mantra:

I give myself permission to be messy.

Evening Reflection:

My feelings didn't need fixing today. They needed space.

Day 186: The Fear of Being a Burden

You learned early to hold it in —
your needs, your sadness, your
overwhelm — because somewhere along
the way,
you feared that expressing them made you *too much*.

But needing care doesn't make you a
burden. It makes you human.
The people who truly see
you will not shrink from
your truth. They'll move
closer.

Morning Reflection:

You are not too much. Your truth isn't a weight — it's a bridge to real connection.

Prompt:

- **Where did I learn that my emotions were "too much"?**

_____
_____
_____
_____
_____
_____
_____
_____

Mindful Minute:

Breathe in compassion. Let it settle over your shoulders like a warm cloak.

Mantra:

I am worthy of care and presence.

Evening Reflection:

I realized today: sharing doesn't make me a burden — it makes me human.

Day 187: Listening Without Solving

Not every wound asks for a remedy. Some just want to be witnessed — to be held in quiet understanding.

You don't have to fix it.
You don't need the perfect words.
Your presence, your patience, your open heart — they are enough.

Sometimes the deepest healing comes from simply being heard.

Morning Reflection:

Sometimes the most healing words are: "I'm here."

Prompt:

- **How can I become a better listener — one who holds space instead of rushing to solve?**

_____
_____
_____
_____
_____
_____
_____

Mindful Minute:

Close your eyes and imagine someone speaking to you.
Respond internally with: *"I see you."*

Mantra:

Holding space is a sacred act.

Evening Reflection:

I practiced listening without interrupting or fixing today. It felt different — in a good way.

Day 188: Vulnerability Isn't Weakness

There's a lie many of us swallowed early
— that to be vulnerable is to be weak.
That strength means silence, stoicism, self-containment.

But vulnerability is not the absence of
strength. It is the presence of truth.
The courage to say, "This is real. This is me."

Letting someone in — into your fears, your flaws, your hopes —
doesn't shrink you.
It expands your capacity to be known, to be loved,
to be human.

You're not soft for opening
up. You're brave.
And you're not alone.

Morning Reflection:

You don't have to be invincible to be respected. You just have to be real.

Prompt:

- **Where in my life do I fear being vulnerable — and what do I think it will cost me?**

_____
_____
_____
_____
_____
_____
_____
_____

Mindful Minute:

Touch your chest and say: *"It's okay to be seen."*

Mantra:

Vulnerability is a strength I'm learning to trust.

Evening Reflection:

I let something true slip through today — and I didn't regret it.

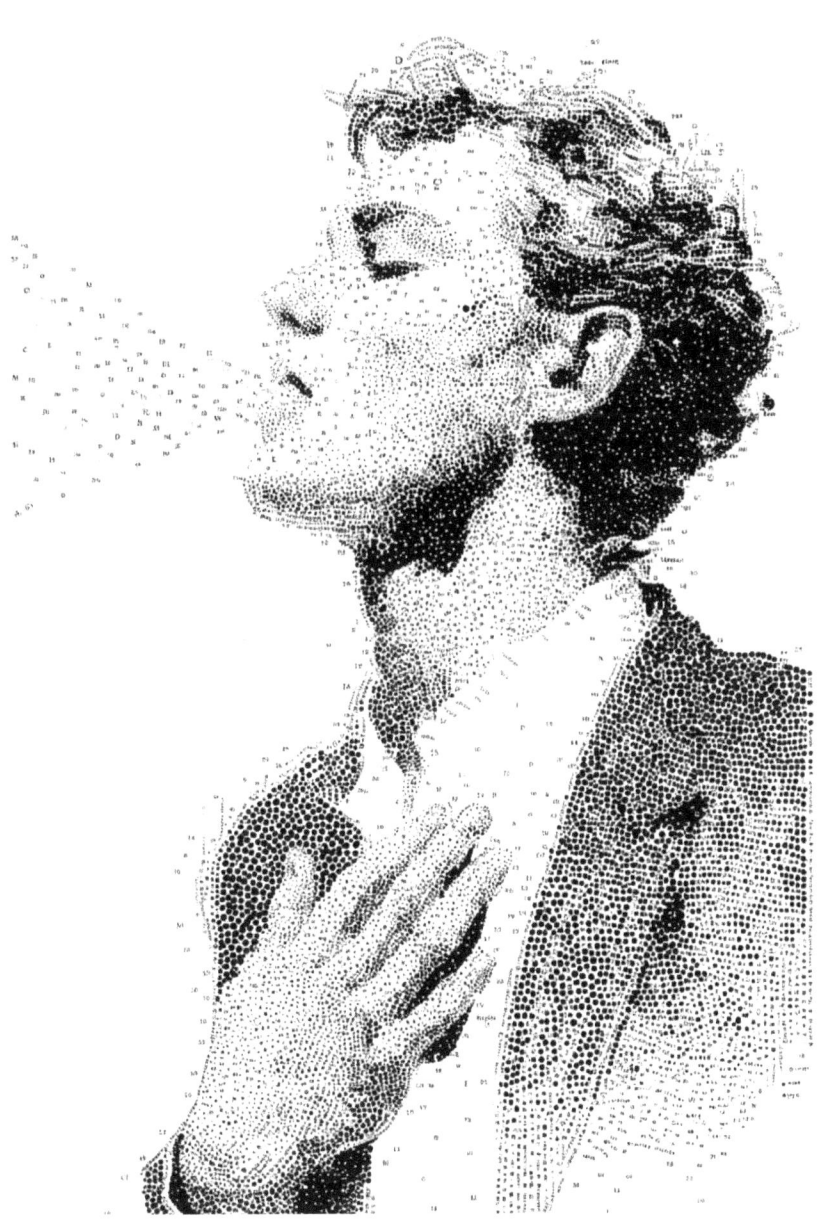

Day 189: Unlearning the Fixer Role

You were taught to solve.
To patch up, provide answers, make it all better.
Somewhere along the way, you believed that love meant fixing.

But not every wound needs a
remedy — some just need room to
breathe.
Not every silence needs filling.
Sometimes presence is enough.

You're allowed to step back from being the
fixer. You can be a witness.
You can be still.
You can love without controlling.

Morning Reflection:

Sometimes fixing is a mask for control — or avoidance.
Healing comes when we let go.

Prompt:

- **When have I used "fixing" as a way to avoid sitting with hard emotions?**

_____
_____
_____
_____
_____
_____
_____
_____

Mindful Minute:

Repeat: *"I choose presence over control."* Breathe slowly and gently.

Mantra:

I am here to feel, not to fix.

Evening Reflection:

I noticed how often I want to fix. And today, I practiced just being.

WEEK 28: Masculinity Without Control

"Masculinity is not about control. It's about presence, awareness, and the courage to stay when you cannot fix."

Let this week be an invitation to release control — not as a sign of weakness but as an act of strength. This is about showing up in relationships and life without gripping too tightly, without needing to manage or mold outcomes. It's about learning how to **hold space** instead of **holding power**.

DAY 190: Let Go of the Grip

You've held on so tightly
— to expectations,
to control,
to the fear of everything falling apart.

But some healing only
begins when your fingers
unclench.
When you surrender the illusion of
control and choose trust instead.

Letting go doesn't mean giving up.
It means giving
space for what is
real,
for what is
next, for what
is true.

Morning Reflection

Where in your life are you trying too hard to control outcomes — your partner's reactions, your child's emotions, your image? The tighter the grip, the harder it becomes to live freely.

Prompt

- **What's one situation I've been gripping too tightly?**

_____
_____
_____
_____
_____
_____
_____

- **What fear would I need to face to loosen my hold?**

Mindful Minute

Breathe in deeply. Clench your fists for 5 seconds. Now release them slowly. Notice how letting go feels — physically and emotionally.

Mantra

I do not need to grip what is not mine to hold.

Evening Reflection

- **Did I notice myself trying to control anything today?**

_____
_____
_____
_____
_____
_____
_____

- **How would it have felt to let go just 10% more?**

DAY 191: Being Present Without Fixing

You don't always need the right words. You don't always need a solution.

Sometimes, the greatest gift is your presence —
quiet, steady, open.

To sit with pain
without shrinking from it.
To hold space
without rushing it away.

Love doesn't always fix.
Sometimes, it simply stays.

Morning Reflection

The people you love don't always need solutions. Sometimes, they just need your **presence** —
grounded, open, and real.

Prompt

- **Who in my life needs my presence more than my advice?**

_____
_____
_____
_____
_____
_____
_____
_____

Mindful Minute

Place a hand over your heart and silently say: "Being here is enough."

Mantra

My presence is a gift, not a solution.

Evening Reflection

- Did I offer space to someone today instead of trying to fix them?

_____
_____
_____
_____
_____
_____
_____

- **How did that shift the interaction?**

_____
_____
_____
_____
_____
_____
_____
_____
_____

DAY 192: Power Isn't Control

We were taught to measure power
by how much we can hold, command, or
control. But real power isn't clenched.
It's not forceful.

It's the calm in
chaos. The stillness
in storms.
The courage to release what we cannot shape.

True power is
knowing you're
secure —
even when your hands are open.

Morning Reflection

Real power isn't in domination or control — it's in owning your energy, being accountable, and choosing your response.

Prompt

- Where have I mistaken control for power in my life?

_____
_____
_____
_____
_____
_____
_____

Mindful Minute

Stand tall.

Inhale with the words "I own my energy." Exhale with "I release control."

Mantra

I am powerful when I am fully myself.

Evening Reflection

- **What did I do today that reflected true power rather than control?**

_____
_____
_____
_____
_____
_____
_____

DAY 193: When Control Feels Like Safety

Control became a shield —
not out of pride, but
protection. It gave you a
sense of order when life felt
unpredictable.

But safety built on
control is a fragile kind
of peace.
One change, and it all crumbles.

Real safety invites
trust. It lets you
breathe,
not just brace.

You're allowed to soften
even when things feel
uncertain. That's where true
safety begins.

Morning Reflection

Sometimes, control is our way of creating safety. But does it truly soothe you, or simply distract you from discomfort?

Prompt

- **How has control acted as my safety mechanism?**

_____
_____
_____
_____
_____
_____
_____
_____

- **What do I fear will happen if I loosen control?**

_____
_____
_____
_____
_____
_____
_____
_____

Mindful Minute

- Scan your body. Where do you hold tension when you feel the need to control?

_____
_____
_____
_____
_____
_____
_____
_____
_____

Mantra

I can feel safe without managing everything.

Evening Reflection

- **Did I choose connection over control today?**

- **How did that feel in my body?**

  _____
  _____
  _____
  _____
  _____
  _____
  _____
  _____
  _____

DAY 194: Holding Space for Discomfort

Discomfort is not
danger. It's not failure.
It's often growth —
showing up in awkward clothes.

We've been taught to escape
it, to fix it, numb it, explain it
away. But healing asks that
we stay.
Not to suffer — but to witness.

Hold space for the
ache, for the
questions,
for the not-yet-figured-out.

It's okay to sit with
it. To breathe
through it.
To trust that clarity often follows courage.

Morning Reflection

To be truly present means to sit with discomfort — yours and others' — without rushing to eliminate it.

Prompt

- **What discomfort do I typically try to avoid or fix too quickly?**

_____
_____
_____
_____
_____
_____
_____
_____

Mindful Minute

Sit in silence for 60 seconds. Let your thoughts rise and fall like waves. Don't change them — just observe.

Mantra

I hold space for what is uncomfortable.

Evening Reflection

- **What discomfort did I witness or experience today?**

_____
_____
_____
_____
_____
_____
_____

- **How did I respond?**

DAY 195: Surrender Isn't Weakness

Surrender is not giving
up. It's giving over.
Releasing the grip on what was never yours to control.

It takes strength to unclench your
fists, to say, "I don't know,"
to trust the unfolding when your mind craves
certainty.

Surrender is soft — but not spineless.
It's the kind of power that knows when to
yield. Not from fear,
but from faith.

Morning Reflection

To surrender is to trust — trust that you are enough, even when life is uncertain and messy. Control says "prove it." Surrender says "believe it."

Prompt

- **What would surrender look like in my current struggle?**

_____
_____
_____
_____
_____
_____
_____
_____

Mindful Minute

Inhale with "I trust." Exhale with "I release."

Mantra

Surrender is strength, not weakness.

Evening Reflection

- **Did I surrender something small or big today? What was the result?**

_____
_____
_____
_____
_____
_____
_____
_____

DAY 196: Rewriting Masculine Power

Power doesn't have to roar.
It can be steady, gentle, and deeply rooted.

We've inherited a script that equates strength
with dominance —
but true power is self-
awareness, the courage to feel,
and the grace to listen.

Masculine power can hold
space. It can protect without
control.
It can lead with
compassion, and still be
firm in truth.

Let's rewrite it —
not to erase, but to evolve.

Morning Reflection

Imagine a masculinity rooted in empathy,
grounded in listening, and expressed through
authenticity. That's real power.

Prompt

- **If I were to redefine masculine power for myself, what values would it be built on?**

_____
_____
_____
_____
_____
_____
_____
_____

Mindful Minute

Visualize yourself standing tall, surrounded by the values you just named. Let them fill your chest.

Mantra

I am redefining power on my own terms.

Evening Reflection

- **How did I embody my definition of healthy power today?**

_____
_____
_____
_____
_____
_____
_____
_____

Week 29 – Safe to Be Soft

Softness is not weakness. It is the courage to feel deeply and still remain open.

Day 197 – The Myth of Hardness

They told you to be hard
— that softness was
weakness, that pain
must be buried,
that tenderness was a threat to your manhood.

But the truth?
Hardness can crack.
It can shatter under pressure,
while softness bends, breathes, and survives.

You were never meant to be made of
stone. You were meant to feel,
to heal,
to hold — and be held.

Hardness is not strength.
Wholeness is.

Morning Reflection:

Growing up, softness may have been framed as a liability.
You were likely told to "man up," "toughen up," or suppress emotions that didn't align with the image of strength. Today, reflect on how that conditioning shaped your relationship with vulnerability.

Prompt:

- **Where did I learn that being soft or emotional made me less of a man?**

_____
_____
_____
_____
_____
_____
_____
_____

Mindful Minute:

Place your hand over your heart.

Take 10 deep breaths and notice how your body feels when you're not trying to guard or brace yourself.

Mantra:

"My softness is sacred, not shameful."

Evening Reflection:

- **Did I encounter a moment today where I allowed softness? How did it feel?**

_____
_____
_____
_____
_____
_____
_____
_____

- **What did it open up for me?**

_____
_____
_____
_____
_____
_____
_____
_____

Day 198 – Armor is Heavy

You learned to wear armor —
tough words, long silences, forced
smiles, the kind of strength that hides
pain.

But armor, though it may
protect, also isolates.
It keeps others out… and you in.

What once kept you safe
now keeps you distant.
And carrying it every
day? It's exhausting.

It's okay to lay it
down. To let someone
see you.
To be met — not just managed.

Because healing doesn't happen behind
armor. It happens in the open.

Morning Reflection:

The armor we wear—emotional distance, stoicism, performance—was likely built to protect us. But now, it might be blocking intimacy and truth. Releasing it is hard, but lightening.

Prompt:

- **What armor am I still wearing, and what do I fear would happen if I laid it down?**

_____
_____
_____
_____
_____
_____
_____

Mindful Minute:

Breathe slowly and feel into your shoulders. Imagine unstrapping invisible armor. Let it drop to the floor with each exhale.

Mantra:

"I can be safe without being guarded."

Evening Reflection:

- **Did I notice any emotional armor show up today?**

_____
_____
_____
_____
_____
_____
_____

- **Did I choose to wear it, or remove it?**

_____
_____
_____
_____
_____
_____
_____
_____

Day 199 – The Language of Gentle Men

Gentleness is not the absence of
strength — it is its highest form.

You were taught to speak
loud, to lead with firmness,
to guard your softness like a secret.

But gentleness is a language,
too. One that says:
"I see you."
"I won't rush you."
"I can hold this moment without breaking."

The world needs men fluent in
kindness. In softness that doesn't
flinch.
In presence that doesn't overpower.

May you learn this language
again. And may it feel like
coming home.

Morning Reflection:

We often speak with force, logic, or avoidance. But language can be gentle and true. How we talk to others— and ourselves—reflects our comfort with softness.

Prompt:

- **What does it sound like when I speak gently?**

_____
_____
_____
_____
_____
_____
_____
_____

- **What would I say differently if I wasn't trying to sound in control?**

_____
_____
_____
_____
_____
_____
_____
_____

Mindful Minute:

Silently say something kind to yourself as you breathe. Notice the internal shift when you replace criticism with care.

Mantra:

"Gentleness is part of my strength."

Evening Reflection:

- **Did I speak or think more gently today?**

_____
_____
_____
_____
_____
_____
_____
_____

- **How did my tone affect the space I shared with others?**

  _____
  _____
  _____
  _____
  _____
  _____
  _____
  _____
  _____

Day 200 – Strength in Feeling

You were told that strength is
silence— that real men don't feel
too much, don't cry,
don't tremble.

But here's the truth:
It takes courage to
feel. To stay present
in pain.
To let joy move through your
chest. To admit, "This matters to
me."

Strength isn't in the shutting
down. It's in the staying open.
In letting your heart break and still choosing to
love.

Feeling doesn't make you
weak. It makes you real.
It makes you whole.

Morning Reflection:

It takes strength to feel deeply. The truth is, most of what we suppress eventually comes out—either in silence, rage, or withdrawal. Today, give yourself permission to feel.

Prompt:

- **What emotions have I been trying not to feel?**

_____
_____
_____
_____
_____
_____
_____

- **Where do I carry them in my body?**

_____
_____
_____
_____
_____
_____
_____

Mindful Minute:

Scan your body for tension. Rest your awareness on that spot and breathe into it. Ask: *What emotion lives here?*

Mantra:

"I am strong enough to feel everything I carry."

Evening Reflection:

- **What feeling did I acknowledge today?**

  _____
  _____
  _____
  _____
  _____
  _____
  _____
  _____

- **What happened when I let it move through me?**

  _____
  _____
  _____
  _____
  _____
  _____
  _____
  _____

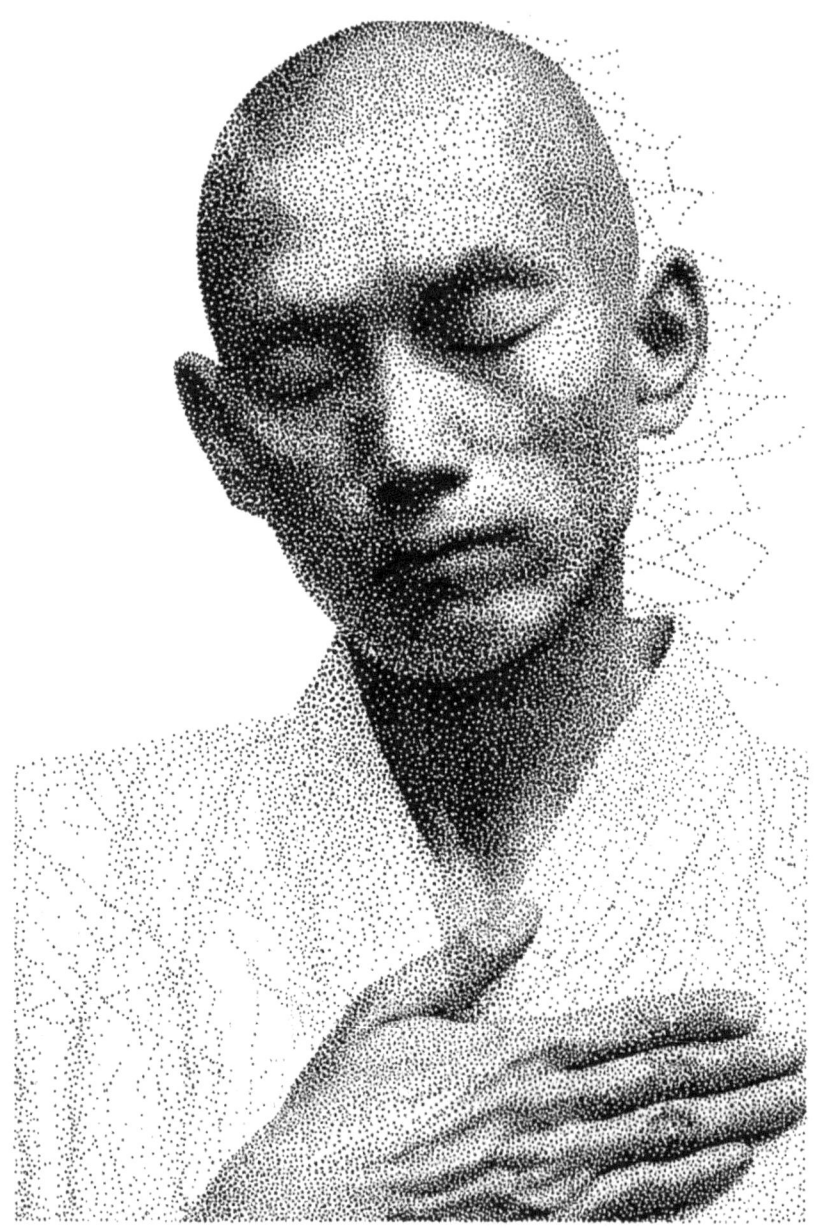

Day 201 – Receiving Without Shame

You've been taught to
give— to show up, provide,
protect.
But receiving? That felt foreign. Undeserved.

Yet healing asks that you open your
hands. Not just to offer,
but to accept.
Kindness. Compliments. Help.

Receiving isn't
weakness. It's trust.
It's saying, *"I am worthy of care, too."*

Let the love in.
Without
apology.
Without shame.

Morning Reflection:

Being soft means allowing yourself to receive: care, love, praise, support. But for many men, this feels uncomfortable—even shameful. Let's unpack that.

Prompt:

- **What support do I usually reject or deflect?**

_____
_____
_____
_____
_____
_____
_____
_____

- **Why does receiving make me uneasy?**

_____
_____
_____
_____
_____
_____
_____

Mindful Minute:

Close your eyes and imagine receiving a compliment or an act of kindness. Let it land. Let it stay.

Mantra:

"I deserve to receive without guilt or apology."

Evening Reflection:

- **Did I receive something today with openness?**

_____
_____
_____
_____
_____
_____
_____

- **What was that like?**

Day 202 – Soft Boundaries

Not all boundaries have to be rigid.
Sometimes, strength looks like
softness— a gentle *no*,
a quiet step back,
a pause to protect your peace.

Soft boundaries honor both you and
others. They say:
"I care. I'm here. But I also matter."

You don't need walls.
You need clarity with
kindness. And space to
breathe.

Morning Reflection:

Softness doesn't mean having no boundaries. It
means creating loving limits without punishment
or withdrawal.
It's strength wrapped in compassion.

Prompt:

- **Where do I confuse softness with weakness?**

- **How can I set boundaries without shutting down?**

Mindful Minute:

Visualize yourself stating a boundary with calm, not force.
Feel the self-respect in that act.

Mantra:

"My softness includes self-respect."

Evening Reflection:

- **Did I uphold a boundary today with softness?**

  _____
  _____
  _____
  _____
  _____
  _____
  _____
  _____

- **What felt different about that approach?**

  _____
  _____
  _____
  _____
  _____
  _____
  _____
  _____

Day 203 – Returning to Your Natural State

Before the proving, before the
performance— there was you.
Unfiltered. Unedited. Unburdened.

Your natural state was not
hardness, but openness.
Not
tension,
but trust.

Healing is not about becoming someone new.
It's about remembering who you
were before the world asked you to
be more, and feel less.

Morning Reflection:

Softness isn't something to become—it's something to return to. You were born soft, feeling, open. The world taught you otherwise. But your softness still lives in you.

Prompt:

- When was the last time I felt fully soft, open, and unguarded?

- What allowed it?

Mindful Minute:

Smile softly. Breathe as if you are safe in your own body.
Say, *"I am home."*

Mantra:

"Softness is my birthright."

Evening Reflection:

- What did I reclaim this week about my softness?

_____
_____
_____
_____
_____
_____
_____

- How can I carry it forward?

_____
_____
_____
_____
_____
_____
_____
_____

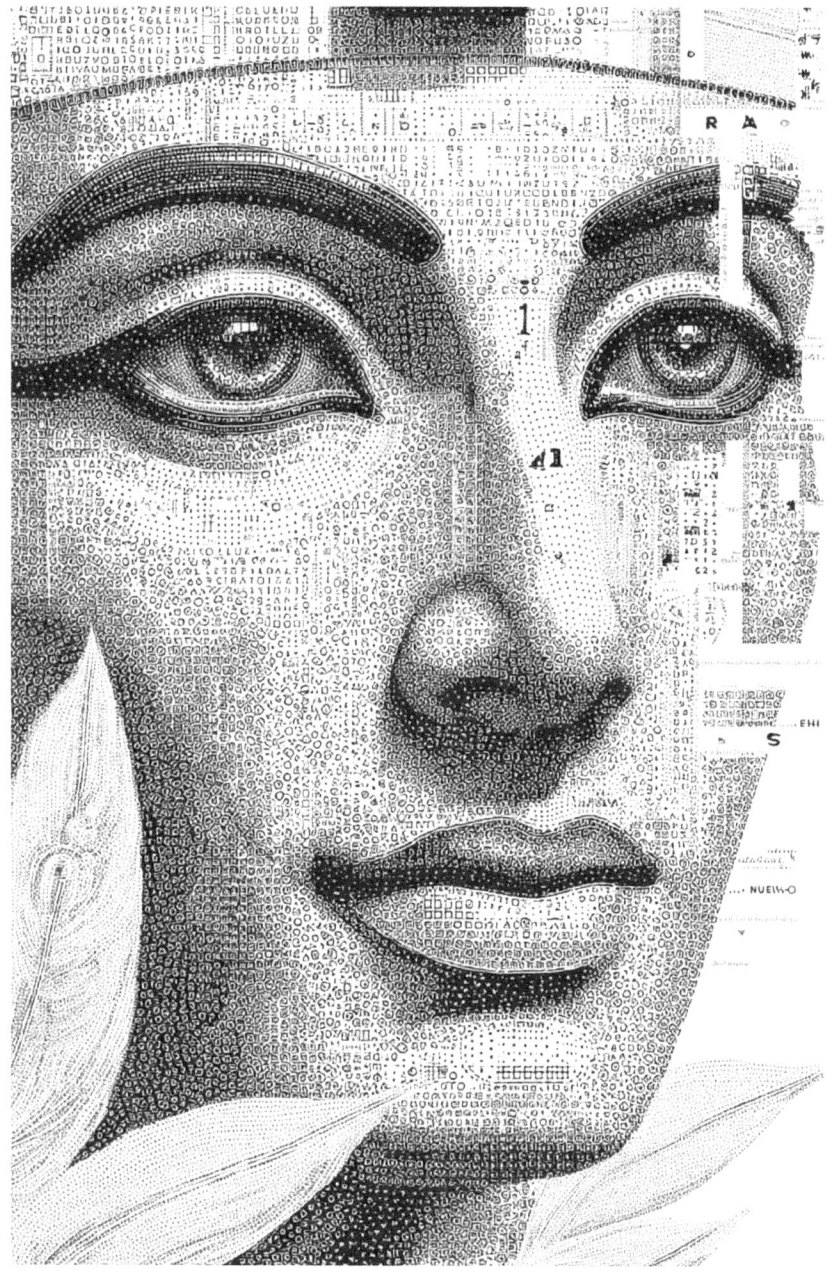

WEEK 30: The Relationship Between Words & Wounds

"Some of the deepest wounds we carry were never physical. They were spoken."

Words shape us — the ones we were told as boys, the ones we whispered to ourselves in shame, the ones we never got to hear. This week, we explore how language has impacted your identity, your emotions, and your sense of safety. It's time to speak with intention and rewrite the inner dialogue.

DAY 204: Words That Built My Armor

Some words didn't just hurt
— they shaped me.
Toughen up. Stop crying. Be a man.

Each phrase, a
brick. Each silence,
a seal.
Until protection became a prison.

But now I name
them, not to relive
the pain,
but to understand the
weight I no longer wish to
carry.

Morning Reflection

Often, we wear armor built from words spoken in our past
— insults, mockery, harsh expectations. Today is a day of reckoning and naming.

Prompt

- **What words from others made me feel small, invisible, or "not enough"?**

_____
_____
_____
_____
_____
_____
_____

- **How did I armor up in response?**

_____
_____
_____
_____
_____
_____
_____

Mindful Minute

With every inhale, say: "I name it." With every exhale, release a memory that still weighs on you.

Mantra

I no longer carry words that were never mine.

Evening Reflection

- **Which part of my emotional armor felt heavier or lighter today?**

_____
_____
_____
_____
_____
_____
_____
_____

DAY 205: What I Needed to Hear

You didn't need
perfection. You needed
presence.

You didn't need to be told to "man
up." You needed to hear, *"I see
you."*
"It's okay to feel."
"You're enough, even now."

Sometimes the healing
begins with offering
yourself
the words no one ever gave you.

Morning Reflection

Sometimes what breaks us is not what was said, but what was never said. We needed affirmation, not silence.

Prompt

- **What did I most need to hear growing up — and from whom?**

_____
_____
_____
_____
_____
_____
_____

Mindful Minute

Speak to yourself now as if you were that child again.

Give him the words you wish he had.

Mantra

It's not too late to give myself what I needed.

Evening Reflection

- **How did I speak to myself today?**

_____
_____
_____
_____
_____
_____
_____
_____

- **Did I say something I always wanted to hear?**

DAY 206: Rewriting My Inner Voice

The old voice was sharp—
critical, impatient,
unforgiving.
It echoed the world's
expectations, not my truth.

But I'm learning to speak
differently to myself now—
with tenderness, with
patience, with the language
of someone worth loving.

This new voice doesn't
shout. It reminds me
gently:
I am allowed to grow slowly.
I am still worthy on quiet days.

Morning Reflection

The voice in your head either uplifts or undermines you.
And the good news? You can change it.

Prompt

- **What is one phrase I often say to myself that is rooted in fear or judgment?**

_____
_____
_____
_____
_____
_____
_____

- **What would a kinder version sound like?**

_____
_____
_____
_____
_____
_____
_____

Mindful Minute

Repeat three kind, supportive affirmations to yourself out loud.

Mantra

I speak to myself with care.

Evening Reflection

- **Was I gentle or harsh in my inner dialogue today?**

_____
_____
_____
_____
_____
_____
_____
_____
_____

- **What do I want to shift?**

  _____
  _____
  _____
  _____
  _____
  _____
  _____
  _____

DAY 207: The Weight of Words

Words can linger longer than
silence. A careless phrase can
carve deep,
while a kind one can stitch what was torn.

I carry some words like burdens,
others like balm.

So now, I speak—
to others, and to
myself— as if every
word
might stay a lifetime.

Morning Reflection

Words can wound — even unintentionally. Today is about owning your impact and acknowledging the weight of what you say.

Prompt

- Have I ever hurt someone with my words — intentionally or unintentionally?

- **How do I feel about that now?**

_____
_____
_____
_____
_____
_____
_____

Mindful Minute

Breathe into your throat and chest. Send warmth to the space where your words rise.

Mantra

My words carry energy. I choose them with care.

Evening Reflection

- Did I speak from love or from fear today?

_____
_____
_____
_____
_____
_____
_____
_____

DAY 208: Silences That Hurt

Not all wounds come from words
spoken. Some come from what was
never said— the apology that never
arrived,
the affirmation that never came,
the comfort withheld in a moment of ache.

Silence can echo louder than
sound, leaving questions,
doubts,
and a longing to be seen.

Today, I choose to give
voice to what I once
needed to hear.

Morning Reflection

What we don't say also matters. Silence can be safety, but it can also be avoidance or suppression.

Prompt

- **What conversation am I avoiding that might be necessary for my healing or someone else's?**

_____
_____
_____
_____
_____
_____
_____

Mindful Minute

Sit with the question: "What truth am I afraid to speak?" Let whatever comes, come.

Mantra

My voice is worthy of being heard.

Evening Reflection

- **Did I hold back anything today that I wish I had said?**

_____
_____
_____
_____
_____
_____
_____
_____

DAY 209: Speaking from the Scar, Not the Wound

There is wisdom in waiting.
Not every pain is ready for
words. Not every ache wants an
audience.

But when healing begins,
the scar tells a story the wound could
not. It speaks with steadiness,
not urgency—
with clarity, not chaos.

I'm learning to
speak when I'm
grounded, not just
when I'm raw.

Morning Reflection

When you speak from an open wound, it bleeds on everyone. When you speak from a scar, you speak from wisdom and survival.

Prompt

- **What painful experience have I healed enough to speak about now — and what would I say?**

_____
_____
_____
_____
_____
_____
_____
_____
_____

Mindful Minute

Touch your heart. Remind yourself: "I survived this. I learned from this. I carry the scar, not the pain."

Mantra

My story is not shame. It's strength.

Evening Reflection

- **Did I share something today that came from healing rather than hurt?**

_____
_____
_____
_____
_____
_____
_____
_____

DAY 210: The Words I Live By

Some words found me when I needed them
most— not loud,
but
steady.
Not
flashy,
but true.

They became anchors in
chaos, compass points in
confusion.

Now, I return to them
often. They remind me:
I am still
becoming. And
that is enough.

Morning Reflection

- **What if you chose your daily words like you chose your clothes — intentionally, with awareness of what they'll carry you through?**

_____
_____
_____
_____
_____
_____
_____
_____

Prompt

- **What three words do I want to live by — and why?**

_____
_____
_____
_____
_____
_____
_____

Mindful Minute

Whisper each chosen word slowly. Inhale their energy. Let them settle into your chest.

Mantra

These are my words. This is my way.

Evening Reflection

- **Did my chosen words guide how I showed up today?**

_____
_____
_____
_____
_____
_____
_____
_____

WEEK 31: Let That Sh*t Go — Codependency

"You were not born to carry what isn't yours. Let go."

Co-dependency isn't just about relationships — it's about losing yourself in the roles you think you must play to be loved, needed, or accepted.

This week, we untangle the silent agreements that taught you to abandon yourself for the sake of others. Freedom begins when you realize your wholeness doesn't depend on who you fix, rescue, or prove yourself to.

DAY 211: The Cost of Carrying Others

Carrying others felt noble—
until I forgot how to carry myself.

I held space, held pain, held
silence, but rarely held rest.

Now, I ask:
Can I still be kind
without self-abandonment?

Compassion should not cost my wholeness.

Morning Reflection

Being the strong one often comes with hidden costs.
Today, we examine where helping others has come at
the expense of your own needs.

Prompt

- **Where have I overextended myself in relationships, and what did I sacrifice in the process?**

_____
_____
_____
_____
_____
_____
_____
_____

Mindful Minute

Place your hand over your chest and say, "I honor my limits." Breathe deeply into that truth.

Mantra

I am not responsible for everyone's healing.

Evening Reflection

- Where did I give from obligation instead of overflow today?

_____
_____
_____
_____
_____
_____
_____
_____

Day 212: Love Without Losing Myself

I once believed that love meant
disappearing— shrinking to fit someone
else's needs,
bending until I broke.

But real love doesn't ask me to
vanish. It invites me to stay—fully,
freely, without apology.

I can love deeply
without losing
me.

Morning Reflection

You don't have to shrink to be loved. Healthy connection doesn't ask you to disappear.

Prompt

- In what relationship(s) have I lost pieces of myself to feel accepted or needed?

_____
_____
_____
_____
_____
_____
_____

Mindful Minute

Visualize yourself standing tall, grounded, whole. No one else's approval needed.

Mantra

I can love without leaving myself behind.

Evening Reflection

- **Did I stay rooted in myself during my interactions today?**

_____
_____
_____
_____
_____
_____
_____
_____

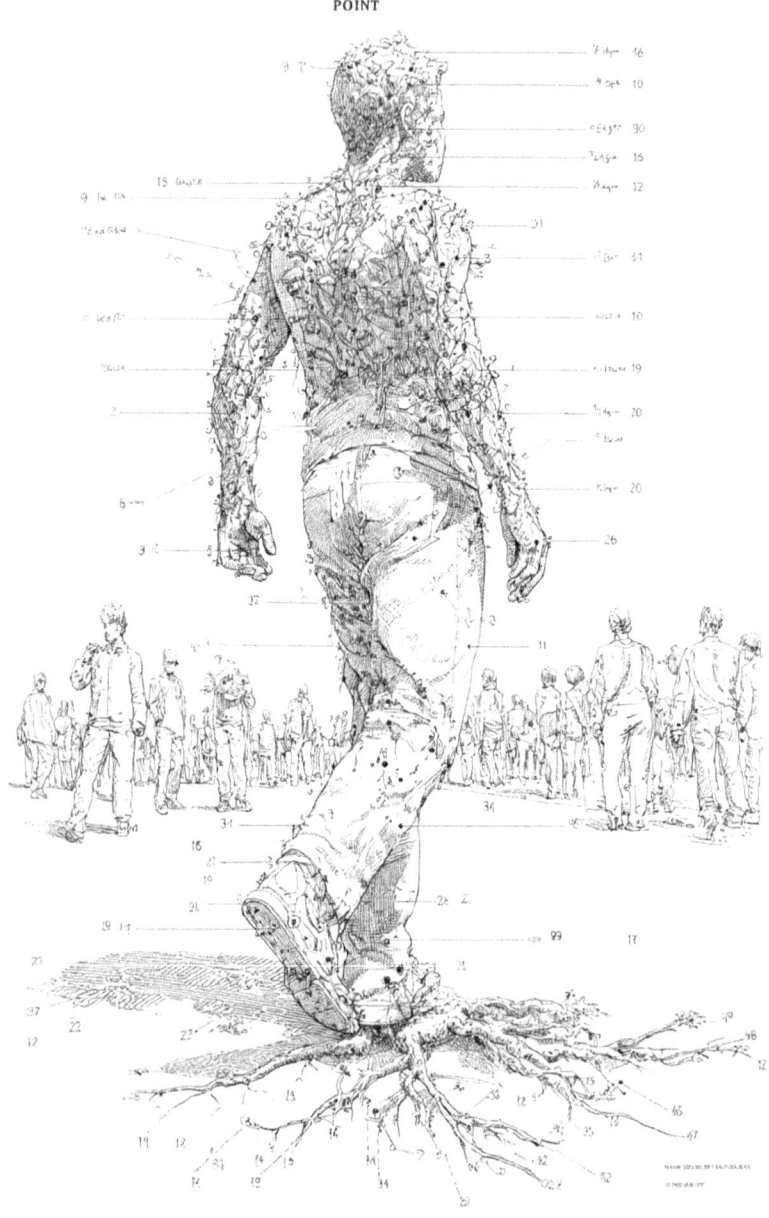

Day 213: When Helping Becomes Hiding

Sometimes, helping is a disguise.
A way to deflect attention from our own
ache. We stay busy fixing others,
so we don't have to face ourselves.

But healing asks for honesty.
Not just with others—but
within.
You deserve the care you so freely give.

Morning Reflection

Sometimes we pour into others so we don't have to face our own emptiness. Helping becomes a distraction.

Prompt

- **Have I ever used helping others as a way to avoid my own healing?**

Mindful Minute

In stillness, ask: "What within me is asking for care?"
Listen without judgment.

Mantra

I deserve the care I so often give.

Evening Reflection

- **Did I tend to my own needs today — or only others'?**

Day 214: Guilt and the Good Guy Script

You were taught to be the dependable one— to smile, say yes, and never make waves.
But sometimes, "being good" came at the cost of being real.

Guilt whispered that your needs were selfish. But needing isn't wrong.
You're allowed to be
whole, not just helpful.

Morning Reflection

People-pleasing is often driven by guilt — the fear of not being "good enough" unless you're giving.

Prompt

- When do I feel guilty for saying no or setting boundaries?

_____
_____
_____
_____
_____
_____
_____
_____

- Where does that guilt come from?

_____
_____
_____
_____
_____
_____
_____

Mindful Minute

Breathe in: "My needs matter."

Breathe out: "Guilt does not define me."

Mantra

No is a full sentence. Guilt is not a compass.

Evening Reflection

- **Did I say yes from guilt or yes from clarity?**

_____
_____
_____
_____
_____
_____
_____

Month 7: Realignment

1. **Where I Feel Aligned Right Now**

- **Which part of your life feels in harmony with who you're becoming?**

_____
_____
_____
_____
_____
_____
_____
_____

Day 215: Untangling My Identity

Who am I beneath the roles I play?
The provider. The protector. The strong one.

It's easy to get lost in what others expect. But identity isn't performance—
it's presence.

And I'm allowed to peel back the
layers to meet the me beneath them
all.

Morning Reflection

Sometimes we confuse being needed with being worthy.
But you are more than the role you play.

Prompt

- **What role have I played in relationships (rescuer, fixer, provider, etc.)?**

_____
_____
_____
_____
_____
_____
_____
_____

- **What would it mean to release that identity?**

_____
_____
_____
_____
_____
_____
_____

Mindful Minute

Repeat to yourself: "I am allowed to be more than who I've been."

Mantra

I am not the role. I am the man.

Evening Reflection

- **Where did I choose authenticity over automatic roles today?**

_____
_____
_____
_____
_____
_____
_____

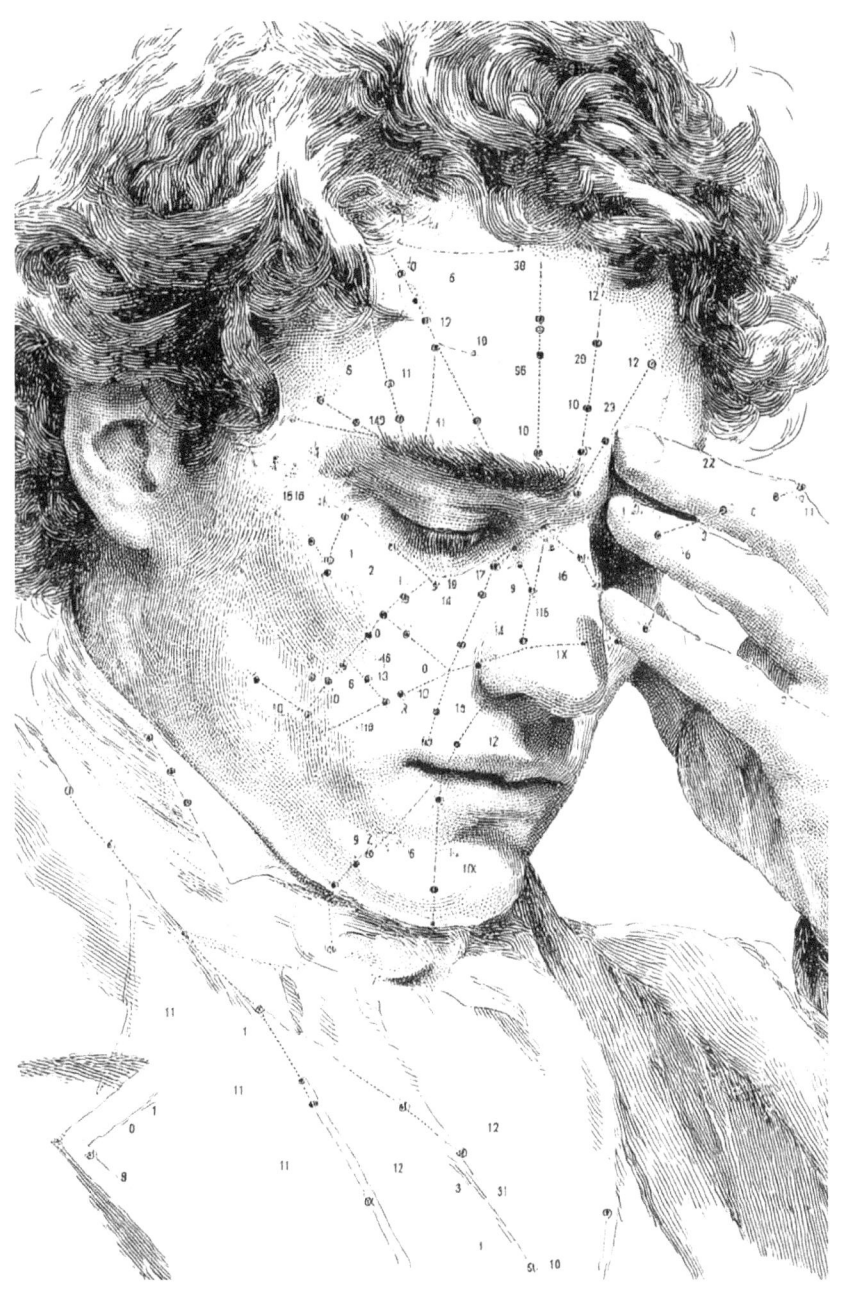

Day 216: The Fear of Being Alone

Aloneness can echo like
abandonment. But sometimes, it's
not emptiness— it's quiet.

It's the stillness where I learn to hear
myself. To sit with my own breath, my own
presence, without rushing to fill the space.

Alone isn't always lonely.
Sometimes, it's the beginning of home.

Morning Reflection

Letting go can feel terrifying — not because of the person, but because of what the emptiness might reveal.

Prompt

- **What am I afraid I'll feel or face if I stop being needed or let someone go?**

_____
_____
_____
_____
_____
_____
_____
_____

Mindful Minute

Sit with the silence. Let the emptiness be a space, not a punishment.

Mantra

Solitude is not lack — it is space for truth.

Evening Reflection

- **How did I experience solitude or independence today?**

_____
_____
_____
_____
_____
_____
_____
_____

Day 217: I Don't Need to Earn Love

Love isn't a reward for performance.
It's not something I hustle
for or barter my worth to
receive.

Real love sees me—not just my
strength, but also my struggle.
Not just my wins, but my weariness.

I am worthy of love,
even when I bring nothing
but my honest, unguarded self.

Morning Reflection

Love is not a transaction. You don't need to perform
to deserve belonging.

Prompt

- **Where have I felt I needed to earn love through effort, perfection, or self-sacrifice?**

_____
_____
_____
_____
_____
_____
_____
_____

Mindful Minute

Speak this aloud: "I am enough, even when I'm not 'doing.'"

Mantra

Love is not earned. I am already worthy.

Evening Reflection

- **Did I allow myself to just be today — without striving?**

_____
_____
_____
_____
_____
_____
_____
_____

WEEK 32: Showing Up as Yourself — Fully

"There is nothing more radical than being wholly, unapologetically yourself in a world that taught you to hide."

This week is an invitation to stop editing yourself for comfort, approval, or safety. The journey of mindfulness is not about becoming someone new, but returning to the man you've always been beneath the performance — whole, honest, and alive. You don't need to wear armor to be powerful.

Day 218: The Mask I No Longer Need

There was a time I wore it so
well— the smile that smoothed
over ache, the strength that
silenced my softness.

It kept me safe.
It won me approval.
But it also cost me pieces of myself.

Now, I choose breath over
performance, truth over perception.

The mask once protected me.
But I've outgrown the need to hide.

Morning Reflection

We've worn masks for so long that taking them off can feel like betrayal — but it's actually the beginning of truth.

Prompt

- **What mask have I been wearing to be accepted
— and what part of me does it hide?**

_____
_____
_____
_____
_____
_____
_____

Mindful Minute

Close your eyes. Inhale: "I am safe." Exhale: "I don't need to perform."

Mantra

My truth is enough.

Evening Reflection

- **Where did I show up without pretense today?**

_____
_____
_____
_____
_____
_____
_____
_____

Day 219: Unapologetically Me

I am no longer shrinking to fit. No longer editing my essence to make others comfortable.

I've spent too long apologizing for my needs, my dreams, my voice.

But every part of me—
even the loud, the tender, the unsure— belongs here.

I am not a performance. I am a presence.

And I take up space—unapologetically.

Morning Reflection

Freedom is living without apology for who you are. You don't need permission to be whole.

Prompt

- **What parts of myself do I downplay to make others comfortable?**

_____
_____
_____
_____
_____
_____
_____

Mindful Minute

Stand in front of a mirror and say aloud: "I am allowed to be all of me."

Mantra

I am not too much. I am not too little. I am me.

Evening Reflection

- **When today did I own my truth?**

_____
_____
_____
_____
_____
_____
_____

Day 220: The Power of Saying What I Mean

There's strength in clarity.
In speaking without the weight of pretense.
In choosing honesty over harmony when it matters most.

I used to wrap my truth in layers—
softening the edges so no one felt uncomfortable.

But I've learned that peace doesn't come from silence. It comes from presence.

Saying what I mean isn't
harsh. It's healing.
It's a declaration:
My voice matters—without apology.

Morning Reflection

Too often, we filter or soften our words to avoid discomfort. But honesty builds real connection.

Prompt

- **Where do I struggle to say what I really mean — and why?**

_____
_____
_____
_____
_____
_____
_____
_____

Mindful Minute

Breathe deeply. On each exhale, release the need to be liked.

Mantra.

My words matter. My voice has value.

Evening Reflection

- **Did I speak honestly with at least one person today?**

_____
_____
_____
_____
_____
_____
_____
_____

Day 221: Taking Up Space

I was taught to
shrink— to be
agreeable,
to be quiet,
to not ask for too much.

But healing reminds me:
I am allowed to exist
fully. To breathe deeply.
To take up space without guilt.

My presence is not a
burden. It is a right.
And every time I choose to stand tall,
I honor the parts of me that once felt invisible.

Morning Reflection

You don't have to shrink to be accepted. Your full presence is not a burden — it's a gift.

Prompt

- **In what spaces do I tend to make myself smaller, quieter, or invisible?**

_____
_____
_____
_____
_____
_____
_____
_____
_____

Mindful Minute

Stretch your arms wide. Ground your feet. Own your space.

Mantra

I take up space with confidence and care.

Evening Reflection

- **Did I allow myself to take up space — physically, emotionally, or vocally?**

_____
_____
_____
_____
_____
_____
_____

Day 222: Being Seen Is Not Weakness

There was a time I believed that hiding made me strong. That if no one saw the cracks, I wouldn't break.

But real strength is letting myself be seen— not just the polished, not just the practiced— but the tender, the tired, the truth.

Being seen isn't
weakness. It's an act of
courage.
It's choosing connection over perfection.

Morning Reflection

Being seen — truly seen — can feel vulnerable. But it's how real intimacy begins.

Prompt

- **What fears do I hold about being fully seen — emotionally, spiritually, or mentally?**

_____
_____
_____
_____
_____
_____
_____
_____
_____

Mindful Minute

Place a hand on your heart and whisper: "It's okay to be seen."

Mantra

Visibility is not vulnerability — it's power.

Evening Reflection

- **Where did I allow myself to be fully seen today?**

_____
_____
_____
_____
_____
_____
_____
_____

Day 223: Permission to Feel, Permission to Be

For too long, I sought permission to feel—
waiting for the world to say it was okay to be
soft, to be unsure, to be overwhelmed.

But the truth is: I don't need permission.
My feelings are valid because they are
mine. My being is enough because I
exist.

To feel is not a flaw.
To be is not a
burden.
It is human. And it is holy.

Morning Reflection

You don't need to earn your emotions. You don't need
to justify your existence.

Prompt

- **Where have I denied my feelings or desires to appear "put together" or in control?**

_____
_____
_____
_____
_____
_____
_____
_____

Mindful Minute

Sit quietly with any emotion present right now. Let it exist without judgment.

Mantra

I don't need permission to feel or to be.

Evening Reflection

- **What did I feel today that I usually push away?**

_____
_____
_____
_____
_____
_____
_____
_____

Day 224: This Is Me — And That's Enough

I've spent years shape-shifting, shrinking, performing— trying to become who I thought I had to be.
But every version built on approval came at the cost of my peace.

Now, I return to myself.
Unpolished. Whole.
Becoming.

This is me.
Not perfect, but present.
And that... is enough.

Morning Reflection

After all the shedding, all the silence, all the reflection — what remains is your truth. That's enough.

Prompt

- **What does showing up fully mean to me?**

_____
_____
_____
_____
_____
_____
_____
_____

- **What does that version of me look like?**

_____
_____
_____
_____
_____
_____
_____
_____
_____

Mindful Minute

Imagine yourself walking into a room exactly as you are — and being embraced. Stay in that image.

Mantra

This is me. And I am enough.

Evening Reflection

- **How did I affirm my wholeness today?**

_____
_____
_____
_____
_____
_____
_____
_____

Week 33: The Brotherhood We Miss

There's an unspoken grief many men carry — the loss of true brotherhood. Not just friendships based on shared activities or banter, but soul-level connections. This week, we explore what it means to be truly seen, heard, and held by other men — and how healing it can be to reclaim those bonds.

Day 225: When We Stopped Hugging

There was a time the arms that once
welcomed us fell still—
not from lack of love, but from learned restraint.

Somewhere along the journey,
touch became taboo.
Affection became
awkward. And warmth
turned silent.

But the absence left a mark.
Because the body remembers what safety once felt
like.

It's not too
late. We can
return.
We can relearn the language of embrace.

Morning Reflection:

- **At what age did physical affection between male friends start to feel uncomfortable?**

_____
_____
_____
_____
_____
_____
_____
_____

Prompt

- **Write about a memory where you wanted closeness or comfort from another man but felt you couldn't ask for it.**

_____
_____
_____
_____
_____
_____
_____

Mindful Minute:

Sit still and place your hand over your heart. Visualize your younger self being embraced — not judged, not rushed. Just held.

Mantra:

"It is safe to seek and offer brotherhood."

Evening Reflection:

- **Did you experience closeness with a male friend today?**

_____
_____
_____
_____
_____
_____
_____
_____

- **If not, what held you back?**

Day 226: Unspoken Grief

Not every grief is loud.
Some sit quietly in the corners of our
lives— never named, never noticed,
but always present.

It's the goodbye we never
got, the dream we buried
quietly,
the love that faded without closure.

Unspoken grief doesn't demand
attention, but it deserves compassion.

Give it a
name. Give it
room. Let it
breathe.

Morning Reflection

- **Is there a male friend you've grown distant from?**

- **What was left unsaid?**

Prompt:

- **Write them a letter (unsent if you wish). Express what you never got to say.**

_____
_____
_____
_____
_____
_____
_____
_____
_____
_____
_____
_____
_____
_____
_____
_____
_____
_____

Mindful Minute:

Breathe deeply and say aloud: "I release the weight of unspoken goodbyes."

Mantra:

"Even in silence, I can heal."

Evening Reflection:

- **What was the hardest part about writing that letter?**

_____
_____
_____
_____
_____
_____
_____
_____

Day 227: Shoulder to Shoulder

Healing doesn't always happen face-to-face. Sometimes, it happens side by side.
In silence. In presence. In shared weight.

Men rarely say, "I'm hurting,"
but they'll stand shoulder to shoulder— on the porch, in the car, during a task— holding space without asking for it.

This is brotherhood.
Not always loud or
emotional, but steady.
Loyal. Present.

Sometimes the deepest
comfort comes not from
being fixed,
but from simply not being alone.

Morning Reflection:

- **Men often bond side by side—through tasks, sports, or building. When was the last time you felt connected that way?**

_____
_____
_____
_____
_____
_____
_____
_____
_____

Prompt:

- **Describe a time you worked alongside another man and felt a deep, unspoken connection.**

_____
_____
_____
_____
_____
_____
_____
_____
_____

Mindful Minute:

Stretch your shoulders gently. Imagine them carrying not burdens, but connection.

Mantra:

"Connection is not weakness — it's resilience."

Evening Reflection:

- **How might you recreate more shoulder-to- shoulder connection in your life?**

_____
_____
_____
_____
_____
_____
_____

Day 228: Rewriting Masculine Bonds

We were taught that closeness had to be
earned, that affection was weakness,
that brotherhood was built only on shared goals or
grit.

But there's a new way emerging—
where we don't just show up for each other in
crisis, but in joy, in rest, in the ordinary.

Where we ask, *"How's your heart?"*
and expect an honest answer.
Where we choose depth over
performance, and presence over
perfection.

Masculine bonds can be tender,
too— honest, healing, whole.
And we get to rewrite what that looks like.

Morning Reflection:

- What have you been taught about male friendships? What needs to be unlearned?

_____
_____
_____
_____
_____
_____
_____
_____

Prompt:

- List the kind of male friendships you desire. What qualities do they have? Openness? Loyalty? Vulnerability?

_____
_____
_____
_____
_____
_____
_____
_____

Mindful Minute:

Inhale slowly and say to yourself: "I am worthy of honest connection."

Mantra:

"Brotherhood is built, not inherited."

Evening Reflection:

- **Did you show up today as the kind of friend you wish to have?**

_____
_____
_____
_____
_____
_____
_____
_____

Day 229: I Miss Him

There's a version of me
that I drifted away
from—
not because he wasn't good enough,
but because life demanded a different face.

I miss his
wonder. His
softness.
His dreams before they were filtered by

fear. I miss the way he hoped without

apology.

But missing him doesn't mean he's
lost. It means I'm ready to
remember.
Ready to return.

Morning Reflection:

Think of a male friend you lost—through time,
conflict, or death. Let yourself feel that loss.

Prompt:

- **What would you say to him if you had five more minutes together?**

_____
_____
_____
_____
_____
_____
_____
_____
_____

Mindful Minute:

With eyes closed, send gratitude to the connection you once had. Let it soften your chest.

Mantra:

"Grief honors love."

Evening Reflection:

- **What memories resurfaced today, and how did they affect you?**

_____
_____
_____
_____
_____
_____
_____
_____

www.ingramcontent.com/pod-product-compliance
Lightning Source LLC
Chambersburg PA
CBHW050254010526
44107CB00003B/315